LIBRARY MANUALS

Volume 4

THE FUNDAMENTALS OF LIBRARY CLASSIFICATION

THE FUNDAMENTALS OF LIBRARY CLASSIFICATION

BERNARD I. PALMER AND A.J. WELLS

LONDON AND NEW YORK

First published in 1951 by George Allen & Unwin Ltd

This edition first published in 2022
by Routledge
2 Park Square, Milton Park, Abingdon, Oxon OX14 4RN

and by Routledge
605 Third Avenue, New York, NY 10158

Routledge is an imprint of the Taylor & Francis Group, an informa business

© 1951 George Allen & Unwin Ltd

All rights reserved. No part of this book may be reprinted or reproduced or utilised in any form or by any electronic, mechanical, or other means, now known or hereafter invented, including photocopying and recording, or in any information storage or retrieval system, without permission in writing from the publishers.

Trademark notice: Product or corporate names may be trademarks or registered trademarks, and are used only for identification and explanation without intent to infringe.

British Library Cataloguing in Publication Data
A catalogue record for this book is available from the British Library

ISBN: 978-1-03-213109-2 (Set)
ISBN: 978-1-00-322771-7 (Set) (ebk)
ISBN: 978-1-03-213272-3 (Volume 4) (hbk)
ISBN: 978-1-03-213273-0 (Volume 4) (pbk)
ISBN: 978-1-00-322840-0 (Volume 4) (ebk)

DOI: 10.4324/9781003228400

Publisher's Note
The publisher has gone to great lengths to ensure the quality of this reprint but points out that some imperfections in the original copies may be apparent.

Disclaimer
The publisher has made every effort to trace copyright holders and would welcome correspondence from those they have been unable to trace.

THE FUNDAMENTALS OF LIBRARY CLASSIFICATION

by

BERNARD I. PALMER
F.L.A.
Education Officer, The Library Association

and

A. J. WELLS
F.L.A.
Editor, British National Bibliography

LONDON
GEORGE ALLEN & UNWIN LTD
RUSKIN HOUSE MUSEUM STREET

FIRST PUBLISHED IN 1951

This book is copyright under the Berne Convention. No portion may be reproduced by any process without written permission. Inquiries should be addressed to the publishers.

In the hope that other authors will be induced to follow our example—and at the risk of denying some librarians the joy of the bibliographic hunt!—we supply the following information about ourselves knowing, as we do, that in large libraries the tracing of such information can occupy the whole time of a skilled bibliographer.

PALMER, Bernard Ira   (1910–   )
WELLS, Arthur James   (1912–   )

PRINTED IN GREAT BRITAIN
in 10pt. Plantin type
BY C. TINLING & CO. LIMITED
LIVERPOOL, LONDON & PRESCOT

TO

W. C. BERWICK SAYERS, F.L.A.

AND

DR. S. R. RANGANATHAN, M.A., L.T., F.L.A.

To the first because we owe him an unpayable debt for his work as a teacher of classification: to the second because he has shown us a way forward.

FOUR PRINCIPLES OF LIBRARY CLASSIFICATION

	WHAT	WHY	HOW
HELPFUL ORDER	An order of arrangement of specific subjects which brings them together in a way most useful to the readers.	Alphabetical order seldom helpful.	By following the order of subjects agreed upon by workers and specialists in their own areas.
	Problems—1. It is relative.	Diversity of interests and multi-dimensional nature of books make for several approaches to same subject.	Alternative location alternative schedules, facet analysis and chain procedure.
	2. It is impermanent.	Development of the field of knowledge produces new subjects and new arrangements.	Recasting of schedules.
MECHANISED ARRANGEMENT	Books, items and entries must be easily inserted or re-inserted in their correct place.	Wasteful to perform an act of classification for every occasion.	Notation which expresses order. Letters, figures, signs, whose rank is defined.
PRESERVATION OF PREFERRED ORDER	New subjects must be inter- or extra-collated in their correct places without disturbing the helpful order.	No classification can enumerate all past, present and future specific subjects.	Decimal fraction notation, octavised decimal fraction notation, faceted notation.
AUTONOMY FOR THE CLASSIFIER	Power of individual classifier to construct his own numbers for new subjects.	Knowledge is advancing, therefore classification schemes always behind wave-front. Without power to construct new class numbers much time wasted awaiting a central committee's decisions.	Scheduled mnemonics, seminal mnemonics, classification as a language of ordinal numbers.

GENERAL INTRODUCTION

IN the general introduction to the earlier volumes in this series, the original editor, Mr. W. E. Doubleday, wrote:

"This new series of Handbooks is intended to supplement the larger Manuals issued by Messrs. Allen & Unwin and the Library Association. . . . (It) is issued independently by Messrs. Allen & Unwin, and the range is sufficiently wide to make the volumes appeal to administrators, librarians, assistants, and students who intend to sit at the professional examinations."

Though the main features in the practice of librarianship are not subject to any great change, many of the details of library administration are under a constant process of development which seeks improvement, e.g. of methods of cataloguing, of book classification, of shelf arrangement, and of service to readers. Those may best be dealt with in small monographs which may be revised at sufficiently frequent intervals.

There is a special need for up-to-date material for the use of candidates preparing for Library Association examinations, either by private study, correspondence course, or, more fortunately for them, at one of the full-time schools of librarianship, and it is hoped that this series will prove particularly helpful to them. It is hoped also that the volumes will be found useful to practising librarians, particularly to those engaged in special departments, or in reorganisation, or revision of library systems which have become out of date.

PREFACE

THE end of all librarianship is the bringing together of the reader and the book or piece of information. All the techniques a librarian acquires are but means to this end. The particular technique with which this book is concerned is classification, and it deals with the search for the most helpful permanent storing order for the books, periodicals, pamphlets, documents and other materials with which the librarian has to work, and for the most helpful order for the arrangement of catalogue entries for those materials.

The increase in the number and importance of special libraries, accelerated by the demands of the Second World War, has brought about a renewed and lively interest in library techniques, and particularly in the technique of classification. The special librarian has to deal with increasingly smaller areas of knowledge, many of which do not fall readily into the convenient groupings of the accepted schemes of classification. The situation has become more fluid, so that librarians must learn not only to fit books into a given scheme of classification, but also how to proceed when faced with a collection of material for which no scheme of classification yet exists.

To public librarians, most of whom work in small libraries with collections of books ranging from 30,000 to 50,000 in number, the problems of classification are not evident. The Decimal Classification seems to serve most of their needs, and they are only conscious of strain when it comes to dealing with new works which are in the vanguard of modern knowledge. This belated realisation of strain is mainly due to the fact that librarians with the requisite degree of maturity and knowledge too frequently have ceased to work in the service departments of their libraries from day to day. Either they are in the technical departments, away from readers and bookshelves, and are quite happy so long as the classification scheme they use provides a place, good, bad or indifferent, for each item; or, they have reached a more exalted sphere where their time is mainly occupied with administrative duties. It is the readers who suffer under bad catalogue- and shelf-order. They feel the inadequacies, but are unaware of just what is wrong, because normally they have no knowledge of classification.

The provision of more trained staff in public libraries to help the reader on the spot would soon cause a clamour for better classification. Special librarians do a greater amount of reference work for their readers, the librarian being constantly consulted by his clients instead of being kept busy with the administration of a number of public buildings and offices. They need good classification schemes in their daily work and are impatient of the inadequacies of the existing schemes.

Even when the public librarian is intellectually convinced of the need for more scientific classification, he is appalled at the size of the task and remains content to muddle through. He does his best to discount all attempts to anticipate problems that are likely to arise. Every public library has some example of an *ad hoc* extension of the adopted scheme produced without reference to practice elsewhere, and every library contains endless examples of decisions taken in placing new subjects which clash with former decisions taken even within the same system.

It is with the object of averting such anomalies that this book is written. An attempt has been made to examine the present position of classification with the object of finding out what it achieves, where it fails, and what steps are needed to increase its value. The object of all techniques is to mechanise processes as far as possible, in order to release for higher purposes the energy that is devoted to their constant operation. A technique must be consciously acquired and demands time and energy for its acquisition. Once acquired, however, it becomes part of the technician and, being absorbed into his outlook, is applied unconsciously thenceforward. Since a classifying mind is essential to a good librarian, classification is one of his foundation studies, and though parts of the subject may appear irrelevant to individual students of librarianship, the subject is one and indivisible and must be grasped as a whole if its purpose is to be fulfilled.

This book is based on a hypothesis which in some respects is not generally accepted. Henry Evelyn Bliss, the author of the Bibliographic Classification whose unparalleled work on the subject of helpful order we largely accept would, we believe, oppose some of our conclusions. In general, his attitude seems to be that knowledge is so diffuse and man's interests so unpredictable that it is impossible to anticipate and provide for new subjects in a scheme of classification. One may only enumerate existing subjects in the light of what he calls the current scientific and educational consensus. He appears to consider that we must be prepared to re-make classifications every generation or so, in order to meet the requirements of new knowledge.

The viewpoint of this present work is based on a different assumption. We fully admit the impossibility of anticipating all new subjects (which are derived composite ideas); but we consider that if we move from the surface level of subjects as they occur in the world of phenomena to the level of the more fundamental urges which move men to the study of subjects, we can discern a pattern in thought activity which coincides with the basic concepts of physical science—matter, energy, space and time. These basic ideas, when "coloured" by the particular subject studied, take on meanings which vary with the "personality" of the subject. Such a pattern enables a classifier to construct a formula which is valid for the analysis of any subject into its fundamental constituent elements. From these elements the complex derived composites that form the subjects of books, etc., can then be built up.

So far as our experience goes, and that of Dr. Ranganathan on whose researches this work is largely founded, this hypothesis is valid. If in the light of future experience it ceases to be valid, we shall see it replaced by another hypothesis which will conform more closely to the facts then known. But for the present we are of the opinion that the hypothesis fully explains the data of library classification and enables us to draw up a set of principles upon which a modern scheme of classification should be constructed.

In this book we make no attempt to construct such a scheme of classification. The following matters only have concerned us:

Firstly, examining in the light of these principles some of the problems which, in our experience, have puzzled students of library classification; secondly, showing how the chief schemes of classification necessarily observe these principles in the main—though the principles may not be explicitly stated; thirdly, demonstrating a method of classifying by the Decimal Classification, based on these principles, which will help to ensure consistent placing and the most helpful arrangement in conflicting circumstances; fourthly, outlining methods of subject indexing and of guiding or featuring the classified catalogue which are mutually supporting and free from the vagaries of individual flair; fifthly, presenting a formula which will enable a classifier to construct for himself classification schemes which will meet the needs of any special subjects.

This book has been written mainly for an audience whose approach to classification is determined by a strong tradition. Because of the strength of this tradition we have felt obliged to work to some extent within its framework, although we feel that this has occasionally rendered difficult the exact expression of our meaning. Our book does not pretend to scholarliness, but is rather an attempt at popularising certain ideas which, despite their importance, as we think, have been largely disregarded. Some of the terminology used is unusual and may even appear gauche, but we are persuaded that the concepts are nevertheless valid.

If our debt to the giants of classification, upon whose work we have so shamelessly leaned, is scantily supported by quotation, it is due entirely to the limitations set upon us. We assume, however, that no one will read this book without also reading the works of Richardson, Sayers, Wyndham Hulme, Bliss, Ranganathan and others of that splendid company of original thinkers.

CONTENTS

	Preface	page 11
	Definitions	16
I.	The Need for Classification	17
II.	Discovering the Most Helpful Order	23
III.	The Process of Division	35
IV.	The Fundamental Concepts Which Underlie Division	42
V.	Phases and Phase Analysis	53
VI.	Notation	60
VII.	Notational Flexibility	67
VIII.	Mnemonics, and Autonomy for the Classifier	76
IX.	The Facet Formula in an Enumerative Classification	82
X.	Canalisation and Practical Classification	89
XI.	The Chain Procedure for Subject Indexing and Featuring	101
XII.	Conclusion, with a Note of Outstanding Problems in Classification	108
	Bibliography	112
	Index	113

DEFINITIONS

The development of our theme has necessitated our using terms with rather special meanings. We therefore give below the definitions of these terms. Most are taken from the vocabulary of Ranganathan.

Analysis —Breaking down a subject into its facets.

Classificationist—One who makes a scheme of classification (called by Bliss classifier).

Classifier —One who classifies (called by Bliss classer).

Classifying —The act of fitting books or other material into an existing scheme of classification (called by Bliss classing).

Division —Breaking down a facet into its foci.

Facet —The whole group of divisions, or foci, produced when a subject is divided according to a single characteristic.

Faceted —A classification is said to be faceted when it provides for the complete exhaustion of each characteristic in turn and the marking off in the notation of each successive facet: hence, also, faceted notation.

Focus (noun) —Any specific division of a subject according to one characteristic: i.e. any single division of a facet.

Focus (verb) —To decrease the extension and increase the intension within any facet, and so arrive at a specific division of a facet.

Form —The method of physical presentation of a subject in a work: the mode of arrangement of contents, or the kind of publication.

Phase —That part of a complex subject derived from any one main class of knowledge.

CHAPTER I

THE NEED FOR CLASSIFICATION

THE problem of the arrangement of a collection of books first presents itself when specific works are likely to be sought by persons other than those who collected the books. The owner of a private library can lay his hand on his copy of Boswell or his French dictionary at will, and requires no systematic arrangement to help him. His guests, on the other hand, will need to scrutinize his bookshelves to find the particular book they want, and the larger the collection the longer the search. Their being guests implies some leisure; but the librarian acts as 'host' to 'guests' who have no leisure for protracted searching through thousands of volumes. He must group his books to meet, as far as is possible, his guests' needs. He must use the principle of orderly arrangement to reduce the cumulative loss of time to successive readers.

Any grouping is better than none at all, if only because it breaks down the whole collection into two or more parts according to some criterion which one can apply mentally to the book one is seeking: e.g. which colour group, which size group or which author group will contain it? Any grouping is better than none, but some are better than others.

The examples just used (colour, size and author) are arranged in order of increasing value as devices for sorting out books. There are comparatively few effective colour groups, at the most a dozen, so that the number of books in each group will be considerable. There are rather more size groups, so the number of items in each group will be fewer. The number of individual authors is legion, so the number of books by each will normally be very few. We see at once that of the three the third grouping would be the most useful in breaking down a collection of books into groups for assisting us in our search for any particular item. We can say, therefore, that of these three criteria for the arrangement of books, that of author appears most potent.

There is, however, another factor also to be considered. The size of the book tells us nothing more than its dimensions, and the colour nothing more than the hues of the binding materials. Also these two criteria are ephemeral: rebinding can change both, the binder may cut edges and may choose a different coloured material for covering his work. The authorship, however, can imply other qualities than merely who wrote it. In a limited degree it can tell us the probable subject of a book. If it is by a known mathematician, it is likely to deal with mathematics, or if by a radio engineer, it is likely to deal with wireless. This is not an infallible test by a long way, but contains a measure of truth. The identity of the author, therefore, can indicate other things besides authorship; that is, it can correlate other qualities. Since we wish to identify books as closely as possible, the greater the potency of the criterion of arrangement the smaller our groups will be, and the more valuable the criterion will be to us. The more qualities the criterion implies (i.e. the more properties correlated to it) the more useful it will be to us.

It must be obvious then that size and colour are of little use in arranging a large collection of books, since the resultant groups still remain too large and too impermanent, and we still know too little about the individual works contained in each group. For our purposes, too, the style of binding is of little value. All such extrinsic qualities fail to help us much and we must seek our useful arrangement elsewhere.

What, in fact, are likely to be useful arrangements? Some memorable and reasonably permanent qualities about books must be sought. We have already seen that author arrangement can be quite useful: we can add to it two other possibilities, arrangement by title and arrangement by subject. Let us examine the possibilities of each.

Author arrangement is related to a permanent feature of a book, but is useless to a reader looking for a book on a special subject if he does not know the literature of the subject. It is a favourite with amateurs, and the old librarians of pre-public library days, for it is a relic of the days when a scholar could know all the major works on his subject and would look for them under the authors' names. Its use in a library of any size today presupposes that bibliographies have been consulted to obtain authors' names. It is a long time, however, before works are embodied in printed subject bibliographies, so that a reader's list of worth-while writers on his subject, if drawn from printed sources, is likely to be out-of-date. Again, a reader may have been able to compile a list of books on his subject but finds none of them in his library. This leads him to imagine, often quite erroneously, that the library cannot meet his demand. His subject may quite possibly be represented by the works of some other author. Author arrangement can only properly respond to an author approach to books. If we widen the scope of the term book to mean all bibliographical material with which librarians work, author arrangement is even less useful. Think of the many publications whose author is GREAT BRITAIN. *Ministry of Agriculture and Fisheries.*

The title of a book is much less stable than its author's name. Apart from the changes wrought by successive editions, by editions in different countries and in different languages, there are the variations produced by usage resulting in shortened titles such as 'Tom Sawyer' 'Robinson Crusoe' and many others. Doubtless a title often conveys the subject content of a book; indeed the title of the monograph or periodical article on a scientific or technical subject is usually a statement of the subject; but in the sciences, where this is most common, title arrangement would result in there being quantities of items under the headings "study", "examination", "analytical", etc., since title arrangement is arrangement by the accident of the first word. This method has the least claim of the three to consideration.

The ordinary reader in the public library has, normally, no special approach except that he wants a book which will interest him. From time to time, however, he finds a need for information, and if his librarian is approachable he asks for subject information. In such cases, whatever he may not know about the book he wants, the reader will know approximately what it is about. This is the subject approach. In the special librarian's experience the most common approach to books is by subject. It is intelligent to anticipate this by arranging the books to meet it. When we go deeper than books, to the level of the article in the periodical, or even the newspaper cutting, subject becomes of prime importance. Scientists and technicians want to know what is being done in their line of work by others; seldom what So-and-so has been writing lately. This level, where the book ceases to be the unit and its place is taken by the shorter article embodying a small but complete idea, is called the documentation level.

Subject arrangement of a collection does not mean that the reader approaching *via* the author is impeded. Subject arrangement breaks a collection down into many small groups, and provided the reader has a general idea of the subject with which his author was occupied in the book he is seeking, the task of picking it out from the small number of other books on the same subject is not an impossible one. In any case, no librarian would seriously consider classifying his library by subject without also providing a classification by author: this latter is normally provided in the catalogue. Indeed, the catalogue should present as many arrangements as are necessary to enable a reader to find his book by whatever approach is most convenient to him.

These are but a few of the more obvious considerations involved in choosing the basis for the arrangement of books. A useful exercise might be to tabulate all the pros and cons of each method, assigning values to them and then to draw up a balance sheet, as it were. Librarians, working empirically over many years, have long since come to the same conclusion as that to which such an exercise would lead: that is to say, that subject arrangement is the most generally useful.

We have been speaking of subject arrangement; but we must stop a moment to consider what we mean by subject. If we ask what is the subject of a book called *Capstan lathe operation*, it can certainly be said to be about engineering: it can also be said to be about machining, also about turning; in fact, it is about a special kind of metal turning. So this book can loosely be said to be about four things of varying intension. We need to be more precise than this in classification: when we use the term subject, we must always mean *specific subject*. The specific subject of a book is that division of knowledge which exactly comprehends all the major factors that go to its making. For example, *A history of steam engines* contains two factors the first, steam engines and the second, historical approach; *Unemployment in Britain in 1930* contains the three factors unemployment, Britain, and the year 1930. It would not be accurate, therefore, to describe the subject of the first example as simply steam engines, nor that of the second as unemployment. We must be quite explicit: we must think always in terms of the specific subject.

When we have decided upon the subject with which a book deals, how are we to arrange it in relation to the subjects of other books? Let us consider another sphere in which subjects are defined and brought into relationship with one another: an encyclopaedia. Here the arrangement is usually (though not always) alphabetical, a useful arrangement if we are dealing with large areas of knowledge like astronomy, mathematics, or physics, which are comparatively few. But when we want to find information about arithmetic, equations or even quadratic equations, we may find that the encyclopaedia we are using merely defines our terms and refers us for fuller information to the more general entry under mathematics. It can be safely assumed that the maker of the encyclopaedia wishes to be as helpful as possible, and that when he refers us to the broader inclusive head he is seeking to be more helpful than he could be by treating each subject separately.

Now let us think again in terms of books on the shelf. If we isolate minor subjects like prime numbers, fractions, etc., and use the encyclopaedia device, namely alphabetical order, to arrange books by their specific subjects, we find these particular subjects widely separated by quite unconnected subjects like heart disease and orange growing. Is this the most helpful order we can find? Consider the subjects, sun, moon, planets, earth, solar system: are they not all parts of the larger subject astronomy? Would they not be better placed somewhere together on the principle that a reader interested in one is likely to be interested in another, or that the books on each are unlikely to exclude completely all that is in the books on the others? If such an arrangement is likely to be more useful, surely we must try to use it. We must try to arrive at as helpful an order as possible, and arrange our books in related groups in the way that the generality of readers will use them. Alphabetical order does not seem to suffice. Some other order, more closely related to the subjects themselves, must be sought.

Here the perceptive reader may well object that what is helpful to one person may not be so to another, that the interrelations of knowledge are so many that to attempt to satisfy one reader will deprive another of the benefits of helpful order: indeed, that what is helpful order on one occasion will be most unhelpful on the next even to the same reader. All this is undoubtedly true, and it is a problem to which we shall have to turn our attention later.

We can only use one order in our shelf arrangement, and that must be the one most likely to be useful to the greatest number of users of the library over the longest possible period. The classificationist is concerned with the general permanent storing order for books. He must leave other orders to be catered for in other ways. Indeed several degrees of permanence in the relations between subjects can be discerned.

There is, firstly, the order which is most commonly accepted as valid over long periods of time: this is the one chosen for the arrangement of books and materials. Next there is the order brought out by special groupings in a dictionary catalogue, or by entries in the subject index of a classified catalogue. Then there is the order produced in reading lists for various needs, individuals and groups of people. Finally there are the many orders reflected in displays made to meet passing interests.

There is, of course, no hard and fast line to be drawn between each of these, but the distinction is clear enough for a working definition. We are concerned in classification with the discovery of the first of these orders and its application to the collection of books with which this chapter began. The time, energy and cost of periodic reclassification must be avoided if possible; we must, therefore, make our order of arrangement that most permanently useful, leaving the others to the care of cataloguers, compilers of reading lists and makers of displays.

The order of arrangement of a scheme of classification must be that which is most permanently useful to the workers in the field of knowledge covered by the scheme.

CHAPTER II

DISCOVERING THE MOST HELPFUL ORDER

THE conclusion we reached at the end of the first chapter is what Bliss[1] had in mind when he stated that the order of a classification should follow that of the scientific and educational consensus. The workers in any field show us by their habits of study the most useful way of assembling material.

But the material with which we work is often very unaccommodating. We are not confronted with a series of books each of which coincides neatly with one of the pigeon-holes of knowledge we can devise. Some books treat a wide subject very generally, others treat a specific subject generally, while yet others treat a specific subject in a special way. Then, again, we often find that the contents of books overflow from one of our pigeon-holes to another, as, for example, in the case of a book on mathematics for engineers.

Given a collection of books consisting of encyclopaedias, general works on major subjects, works on major aspects of some of these subjects, and detailed works on minor included subjects, how is it best to arrange them if they are to appear in the most helpful order? Would the first group of books deal with the microbiology of cellulose, the second group with chemistry, the third with science, and so on? It is doubtful if anyone would begin that way round, that is, with a very specific subject working up to the more general. The reasonable course would seem to be to begin with the more general works, which give an overall picture, and proceed by increasing specificity and complexity. Then the reader who wants something about a topic in chemistry may take up a general encyclopaedia for a brief survey of the subject, a general work on science for a more detailed study, a manual on chemistry for a closer study, and so

[1] Bliss. Organisation of knowledge in libraries.

on down to the monograph or periodical article on the most minute part of the subject.

If the books are arranged in such an order, beginning on the left-hand side of the shelf, the reader should be able to light readily on just that part of a shelf of books which seems appropriate to his needs, and to move left or right to the exact spot, helped by the order. That is the aim of the maker of a classification scheme: to lay the books out in the order most helpful to the reader.

Helpful order can be defined as that which displays subjects in such a way that a person approaching a group of subjects at any point is led by the order itself to the specific subject he needs. We are brought to this conclusion by observing the habits of readers in seeking their subjects. Firstly, most people do not think in terms of specific subjects, but in terms of the more general subjects which contain them; for example, the request for 'a book on birds' proves to be a desire for information on the aerodynamics of bird flight. Secondly, readers require other related material in most cases: for example, it is unlikely that the man who today asks for information about growing onions will not later require similar information about beans and cabbages. Thirdly, many people cannot accurately define a specific subject until actually confronted with it; for example, the specific subject implied in the question 'why do leaves fall?' is botanical ontogeny. Fourthly, many specific subjects are only to be found with material of a more general nature; for example, the information on preparing ground for growing peas will be found in a general work on gardening.

An order which itself leads to the specific subject sought, no matter what the point of approach, demands a system which arranges subjects in an order of decreasing extension so that the general subject, which may include material on the specific subject, is followed by the specific subject itself. Specificity is a relative matter, however, and we have to fix on an order which gives increasing specificity, no matter how complex the subjects that have to be arranged.

The order which appears to be the most useful is to put the general works first, followed by works on general subjects treated specially, then by works on special subjects treated generally, and lastly by works on special subjects treated specially[1]. Examples may make this clear.

1. The general treated generally .. An outline of medicine.
2. The general treated specially .. Surgery: a manual for the general practitioner.
3. The special treated generally .. The stomach: a general handbook.
4. The special treated specially .. Surgery of the stomach.

The arrangement of books demands that we give names to the groups into which we divide them, so that we can refer to them conveniently. We call some books works on science, others works on art. The names thus given are called the terms of the classification. The subjects which these terms represent obviously vary in scope, and this variation is called the extension and intension of the subjects. A wide subject is said to have great extension, since it extends over a wide area of knowledge. At the same time we know little about the detailed contents of the subject, and we say, therefore, that it has little intension. As we move down from wider to narrower subjects, it is obvious that the terms are denoting concepts of increasingly smaller extension, but as they are dealing with more and more definite subjects, we know more about them and we can say that the intension of the concepts denoted by the terms increases.

If we look at the schedules of the Decimal Classification, at, say, class 500, science, we observe that this class covers a wide variety of subjects but tells us little about them save that they share the common approach to knowledge which we call scientific. The term, then, denotes a subject which has great extension but small intension. Looking down the schedule, we find 510, mathematics. This term covers a narrower subject than science in general, being but part of it, but we can infer more about its contents. We know, that is to say, that it deals only with the relationships between abstract numbers. We can say that it is of smaller extension than science in general, but that its intension is greater. If we continue to examine the

[1] Bliss. Bibliographic classification: introduction.

mathematics schedule, we come to terms denoting subjects of even smaller extension, but they become more and more definite in meaning, because the intension of the subject they denote increases.

Sayers, basing his theory of classification on Aristotelian logic, stated that classification should proceed from terms of great extension and small intension to terms of great intension and small extension. [1] A little thought soon shows us that this is a formal statement of the conclusions to be drawn from the examples given below.

We are, of course, only at the beginning of achieving helpful order. In effect, what we have agreed to do is, having decided upon the relationships of all the subjects which will appear in our schedule or list of terms, to arrange that the more general ones shall precede the more specific. Our next problem is that of arriving at the order for relatively equal subjects.

Supposing we have been given the task of organising a library of books and articles on building work, how would we set about arranging them?

We should begin probably by grouping together the works on bricklaying and masonry, those on tiling, those on carpentry and so on through all the major trades concerned in building. This we should do, in Bliss's phraseology, because of a scientific and educational consensus, not in the narrow sense, but in a wider one which also includes a technological consensus. Because the books are most useful in trade groups, we should bring them together thus from the generality of books. We should use the building operation as a polarising agent in our grouping.

It is possible to look at this from a different viewpoint, however, and to arrive at the same conclusion. This time we should start from the assumption that we have at our command all the books on building, and we wish to break them down into convenient groups, instead of bringing groups together to make a whole. We therefore look for a principle by which to divide all books on building, and again we select the building operation, thus arriving at the same result.

[1] Sayers. Introduction.

There is no fundamental difference between grouping books together conveniently according to some established 'consensus' and dividing a mental conception of an area of knowledge according to the most potent principle. The only difference is one of approach. The first is that of the practical man who works by rule of thumb and corrects his errors as he goes; while the second is that of the theoretical man who, observing the results of the efforts of the practical man, works according to the general rules which he has deduced from them.

The practical man, then, first shelves the groups as they occur, and labels each in some such way as:—MASONRY, CARPENTRY, TILING, PLANNING, PLASTERING, etc. He may then gather the results of his labour together and label the book cases which house them with the words 'Books on Building'. If he went on to commit his arrangement to paper, we should call this his classification schedule.

His theoretically-minded counterpart, however, begins by writing down the term denoting the whole contents of the collection, and after some cogitation adds 'divide by the building operation,' and then lists the groups into which he will later divide his books.

The choice of characteristic by which to divide is not a light matter. It must prove essential to the purpose; that is, break down the books into the right sort of groups, and it should take into account (or correlate) as many qualities of the subjects of the books as possible. There are so many aspects to any subject that it is not possible to represent them all; nor is it necessary. Only those essential to the purpose in hand need be considered.

The resultant divisions may either be set out as a list, thus:—

BUILDING
Planning
Masonry
Tiling
Carpentry
Plastering
Glazing

or shown as a sort of 'genealogical tree', thus:—

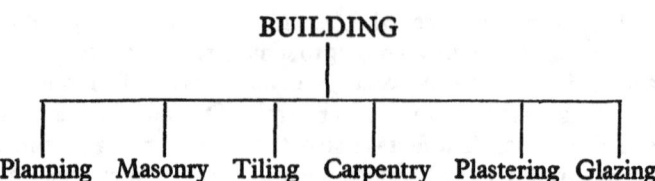

The list form shows us no more than the contents of the class Building (henceforth we shall cease to say 'books on', as it can be assumed that we are dealing with records of knowledge in the subjects quoted). The genealogical tree form shows us something additional, that each of the operations listed is of equal rank in the division. That is to say, each derives directly from the general task of building, and is not a subdivision of any of the others. Since none of them is subordinate to another, they must be co-ordinate groups: that is, equal in rank. It is one of the advantages of theory that it can help us to see more of a subject at a glance. Henceforth, we shall work in this book from a basis of theory, whilst admitting that, in time, the practical approach might give the same results.

We have, then, set out a number of co-ordinate groups in an array under the general heading. Look at them again, and ask yourself if the order in which they are set out is the most helpful to be found. Remember that any given number of objects can be arranged in $1 \times 2 \times 3, \ldots \times$ the given number of ways, and this gives us a vast number of possible orders. The accidental order in which we first wrote down the divisions is not likely to be the best order for our purpose. Perhaps alphabetical order would be better, or one based on the order in which the operations are applied to the actual erection of a building.

The arranging of a library, therefore, involves two steps: firstly, the breaking down of a class into a number of co-ordinate divisions by the consistent application of a given principle (a characteristic of division) and secondly, the assembling of the resultant series of co-ordinate divisions into the most useful order.

In the example used above, the subject itself provides an easy answer to the problem of choice of order. In other cases the

DISCOVERING THE MOST HELPFUL ORDER

answer is not so obvious. The question of what order to choose has already been examined by Ranganathan,[1] and if we accept his findings we need not do the job empirically every time. We shall here accept the result of his examination of the existing schemes of classification and shall proceed on the assumption that there are seven possible orders in array. These are as follows:—1, Canonical (i.e. complying with custom): 2, Evolutionary: 3, Spatial contiguity: 4, Chronological: 5, Alphabetical: 6, Increasing complexity: 7, Categorical (an *ad hoc* order which will serve until one of the others seems more applicable).

When confronted with the task of dividing up a class we must first of all discover the characteristics which will break the class down into the divisions which will be most useful for our needs, and then arrange the resulting co-ordinate classes according to that order out of the seven given above which will prove most useful.

If, however, our collection of books on building is large, we shall find that we have not gone far enough. Indeed, in any case we shall find some items that do not fall into the category of books on building operations. Some will have to do with the materials of building, for instance. Having exhausted the possibilities of the operation characteristic, we must seek another characteristic to apply which will divide our small groups into smaller ones, and take care of some of those books which will not fall into the *operation* groups. We therefore turn to material as a characteristic of division and repeat the formula, as before. We may well find that many of the divisions under the second characteristic will apply to more than one of the divisions under the first. We shall then be in a position to break down the operation groups into smaller ones which relate to operation plus material. The process of division demands that we take one characteristic and exhaust its possibilities, then take another and do likewise, and so on till we reach the smallest groups convenient for our use. At each step we shall get an array of divisions co-ordinate with one another, and these must be put into helpful order each time. Of course, what constitutes helpful order among the array produced by the application of the

[1] Ranganathan. Elements.

first characteristic may not do so in the array arrived at by the application of the second.

How can we know that we have exhausted the possibilities of any characteristic? In Shakespeare's day the application of the characteristic operation to the class building would not have given us electrical work as a co-ordinate class with carpentry. In Roman times it would have given us plumbing, though not in medieval times because that art was lost, and only appeared again in modern days. There may be other building operations in days to come of which so far we have no cognisance. In writing out our list or schedule of the divisions of building, then, we must be prepared for future additions. We can only be exhaustive in our division as far as our knowledge goes, and make a note that we must provide for the future. If, however, we take care to make clear the basis on which we have divided: if we state our characteristic of division, our successors will know how to carry on our work.

We must exhaust the possibilities of one characteristic before applying another: this is most important. What happens if we do not observe this rule, but try to apply two characteristics simultaneously, or at random?

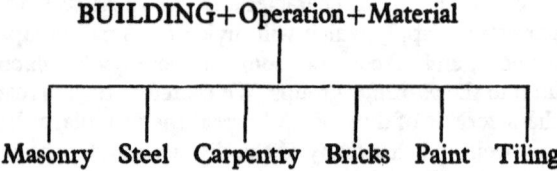

We should get a heterogeneous array of subjects derived from building, some *via* one characteristic and some *via* another; but we cannot claim that they are co-ordinate divisions because some are dependent for their very existence upon the existence of others. Books on making roof-trusses might be placed with carpentry or with steel. When this happens, and no classification has avoided it entirely, it is called cross division.

Cross division could be avoided by observation of the rule that characteristics used as the basis of division must be used with consistent meaning and applied in a stated order, the possibilities of each characteristic being exhausted before the introduction of the next.

To return to our example of books on building: what does the list of building operations show us? It reveals that aspect or *facet* of the subject Building which is related to the operation concerned. A second list could reveal that aspect or *facet* of Building which is related to the materials used. From this we realise that every subject has one or more aspects which correspond to the characteristics used as a basis for division. The sum total of the divisions of each aspect we shall call a facet.

If we turn to class 942, History of England, of the Decimal Classification, we shall find a list of period divisions. These are based on the characteristic Chronology, and we can say that they constitute the chronological facet of the History of England. Printed after these period divisions we find another set of divisions which relate to the different areas of England. These are based on the characteristic Geography, and we can say that they constitute the geographical facet of the History of England.

In class 940–999, Modern History, of the Decimal Classification, the two facets are very easily distinguishable, because the chronological facet always follows the geographical facet in the class number, and is separated from it by a zero. Examples:—
(1), 942·05 is History of England in Tudor times: (2), 952·02 is History of Japan in the Shogun period: (3), 994·02 is History of Australia in the Settlements period. These can be analysed and set out thus:—

History		Geographic Facet (Space)	Chronologic Facet (Time)	
(1)	9	42 England	0	5 Tudor period
(2)	9	52 Japan	0	2 Shogun period
(3)	9	94 Australia	0	2 Settlements period

It is worthy of note at this point that although they are printed in the schedules *after* the period divisions, the further geographic subdivisions which break the various countries down into smaller areas are given a notation which is inserted *before* the zero which denotes the period.

The method of reduction to constituent parts which was

used in the examples above is called *facet analysis*, which simply means the analysis of a specific subject into the facets produced by the application of different characteristics. It can be applied to any scheme of classification, and is the best method known of checking the correctness of a class number arrived at by a classifier. Incidentally, it also reveals ordinal deficiencies in the classification scheme in use. The constituent parts are like chemical elements: they can be combined in various ways to produce a large number of derived composites. Most specific subjects are derived composites built up from fundamental constituents drawn from two or more facets of the main subject.

Turning now to the diagram opposite which shows a number of divisions based on a single characteristic, we find that the analysis contained in it gives us four steps of increasing intension and decreasing extension in isolating History of the City of London from the general class History of Europe, and they are all based on the geographical characteristic. How shall we describe this process of decreasing the area of our interest? We can say that the term London County denotes a subject of less extension than the term England but of greater extension than the term City of London; but that does not describe the process so much as its effects.

If we think of the map of Europe, we focus our attention on that part of the world. If we restrict our attention to smaller and smaller areas, we say that we focus our attention on those areas. There is no doubt that *focusing* admirably describes the mental process of narrowing down one's interest from major to minor divisions of a facet of any subject. We can derive from it the term *focus* (noun) to describe any one of these divisions. A book may have many foci in the facet under consideration, or it may be so general as not to specify any one of the foci, but pervade them all. In the first case we can say that it is multi-focal, and in the second that its focus is diffuse.

The terms facet and focus are relatively new to classification; but they are very important, as they give names to phenomena in this subject which have so far lacked definition, and so eluded the grasp of students. They form a valuable tool for the

A Diagram Showing the Division of the History of Europe by the Geographical Characteristic

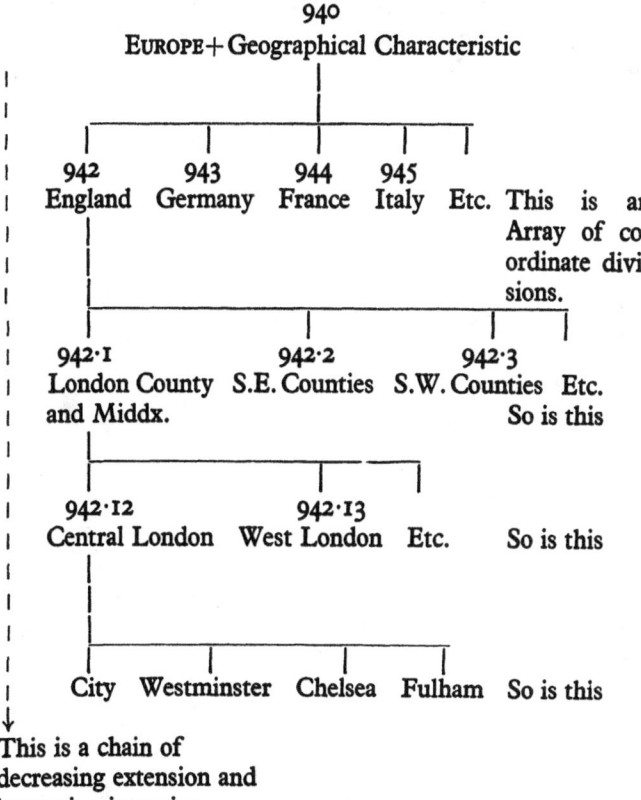

Explanation of the Diagram.

The relationship between the subjects read from left to right is that between equals: they are co-ordinate subjects set out in an array. The relationship between the subjects connected by vertical lines is that between superiors and subordinates. They are a series of subordinate subjects set out in a chain. Every subject which appears in the above diagram is a focus of the geographical facet of the History of Europe.

analysis of the achievement and limitations of past schemes. What we hold to be more important is that their recognition is fundamental to future research into classification, and through them it is possible to know the form which a future scheme of classification should take.

CHAPTER III

THE PROCESS OF DIVISION

WE have been considering so far the achievement of helpful order, and we have found it reasonable to arrange like subjects with like. Arrangements may be made in accordance with the needs of the workers within a given field either by the method of trial and error (grouping) or by the application of observed principles (analysis).

We have reached the conclusion that division and grouping are both ways of approaching the same problem. In classifying we begin with a species and assign it to its genus, whereas in making a scheme of classification we begin with a genus and divide it into its species. The classificationist (the maker of a scheme) uses the principle of division in producing his schedule and gives a symbol to each·of the divisions he has listed: the classifier assigns books to various divisions and puts on each book the symbol appropriate to its subject. As a result of the work of these two persons, the task of classifying which takes place every time a heterogeneous collection of books is shelved, is rendered comparatively simple and mechanical

It is clear that it is impossible to list all subjects, past, present and future, so that books will appear upon subjects which are not shown in the schedule, and when this occurs the classifier must assign them to places within the helpful order of the scheme. When he does this, and he does it quite often, he takes on the functions of the classificationist. Consequently, he requires to know the principles upon which the scheme is based, and must have a knowledge of the processes of division. Indeed, he will need to know more than this if he is to carry out properly the job of fitting every subject into its proper class. The understanding of division is, then, a prerequisite of classifying.

The classification which is found in the older works on logic also concerns itself with the processes of division. It aims at mutual exclusiveness as between one species of a genus and another, as is illustrated by the tree of Porphyry, in which a species is derived from a genus by the discovery of a difference, so that each genus is shown to divide into two species, one of which possesses the difference and the other does not. This sort of division is called dichotomous and is quite useless for our purpose.

The aim of library classification is to show a general picture of the relationships of knowledge, and this demands so much simplification that cross division rather than mutual exclusiveness of subjects is a more common result. Other methods have to be devised to overcome cross division. These other methods are refinements of notation, cataloguing and special displays.

When the classificationist makes his scheme he wants to show all the co-ordinate classes that can be derived from the major inclusive class in one operation. He is not content to go through the process of dichotomy, deriving one species at a time by seeking the difference again and again. He looks instead for some quality of subject which all the books in a class possess in varying degrees or measure, or in different ways, and uses this quality as a criterion of arrangement. The subject Education, for example, might be divided up according to the class of persons to be educated, in which case the resultant divisions would be something like this:—

>   Pre-school child
>   Elementary stage (5–11)
>   Secondary stage (11–18)
>   University stage (18–22)
>   Adult stage (22–   )

From another viewpoint, we may divide Education according to the problems it propounds, the resulting divisions being something like this:—

>   Curriculum
>   Teaching methods
>   Provision of buildings.

It is essential to realise that this process of division by successive characteristics is fundamental to all classification schemes, although it is only glimpsed occasionally (as under 942, where division by the chronological and geographical characteristics are clearly provided for) in the Decimal and other classification schemes which enumerate specific subjects. These facets of a subject which coincide with characteristics of division are to be found in all schemes, but they are embodied in a mass of enumerated specific subjects and therefore hidden, and must be consciously sought before they reveal themselves. Enumerative classifications list composite subjects built up from a number of basic ideas. Faceted classifications list the basic terms, and leave the building of derived composite terms to the classifier.

This will be made clearer by examining a very simple enumerative scheme for the arrangement of a few books on religion, and deciding what are the characteristics of division used in it.

> RELIGION: General
>   Founders of religions
>   Sacred books
> CHRISTIANITY
>   Christ
>   Bible
> MOHAMMEDANISM
>   Mohammed
>   Koran

This small schedule can be seen to be based on the use of two characteristics—the religion involved and the religious activity involved, (by activity is meant the challenge of the subject to our faculties). The characteristic *religion involved* gives rise to two divisions: Christianity and Mohammedanism. The characteristic *activity* gives rise to two divisions under the general heading, and two under each of the religions named. We can, then, express the above schedule in terms of its basic concepts thus:—

RELIGION	(Religion involved)	(Activity involved)
	Christianity	Founder
	Mohammedanism	Sacred books

remembering that the divisions under the second characteristic named can be applied to each of the divisions under the first.

If you can see how the first of these schedules is built up on the basis of the second, try now to see if you can derive a schedule of the second type (which we call a faceted schedule) from a section of the Decimal Classification, or from any other scheme with which you are more familiar. The Decimal Classification class 920, for example, is divided by the characteristic of the life's work of the biographee; class 800 is divided first by language, then by form, then by period, within which a few selected authors are named. We can make a formula for literature thus:—

LITERATURE (Language) (Form) (Period)

We can check the accuracy of this by taking a few subjects and classifying them by the Decimal Classification.

1. Literature in general . all facets diffuse 800
2. History of literature . language and form facets diffuse 809
3. Collected poetry .... language and period facets diffuse .... 808·81
4. English literature .. form and period facets diffuse 820
5. English poetry ..... period facet diffuse 821
6. Elizabethan poetry .. all facets specified .... 821·3

It is not often so simple as this with the Decimal Classification; but it is nevertheless possible in every part of the schedules. It must be remembered, however, that the Decimal Classification by the nature of its construction and growth is not often consistent in its use of a characteristic, and frequently introduces a second characteristic before finishing with the first.

When the technique of discovering the characteristic used, and of recognising the facets that correspond to them has been acquired, it will be found possible to put a finger more easily upon the weaknesses of the Decimal Classification and of any other scheme, for the principles are equally good for all.

We are now in a position to see the importance of an understanding of division for classifiers. We know that we can divide the class literature according to three different characteristics.

THE PROCESS OF DIVISION

These we can apply in any of six orders: i.e., $1 \times 2 \times 3$, since there are three characteristics. Having chosen one order, however, we cannot use any other. Dewey has chosen to divide by language first, so that all English works are together, separated from all the French works. But a student of poetry may require all the books in verse, irrespective of language, or another reader may want to see everything produced in the 16th century, regardless of form or language. Such people the Decimal Classification will not serve. This is the problem that lies behind helpful order: which is the best arrangement for general purposes, and how are the others to be served?

We saw in the last chapter that when we divide a subject according to a given characteristic, we produce an array of co-ordinate divisions. We saw also that each of these divisions could again be divided, producing further arrays of divisions. Each time we take such a step in division we necessarily produce an array of divisions (although the array may be limited to only two co-ordinate divisions). At the same time we observed that each step in division was producing a link in the chain of subordinate divisions with respect to the subject from which it first derived.

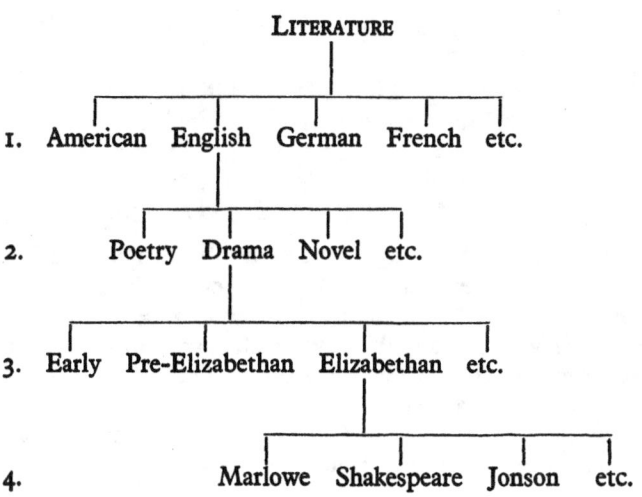

This diagram shows this principle being worked out in literature. We show four arrays of co-ordinate subjects, each array being subordinate to the one preceding it. If we begin at Shakespeare and work vertically upwards we come to the general heading Literature, and we can describe the connection between General Literature and Shakespeare as a *chain* of successively subordinate divisions.

It thus becomes manifest that in book classification division is two-dimensional, for every time we produce an array of co-ordinate divisions we produce an equal number of chains of subordinate divisions. In the example above there are three chains of two links each:—

array 2. Literature   Literature   Literature
          English   English   English
          Poetry   Drama   Novel

the first link being common to all. There are three chains of three links each:—

array 3. Literature   Literature   Literature
          English   English   English
          Drama   Drama   Drama
          Early   Pre-Eliz'n   Elizabethan

the first two links being common to all. There are three chains of four links each:—

array 4. Literature   Literature   Literature
          English   English   English
          Drama   Drama   Drama
          Elizabethan   Elizabethan   Elizabethan
          Marlowe   Shakespeare   Jonson

the first three links being common to all. The unspecified divisions labelled 'etc.' at each step have not been counted. We must bear in mind then the fact that every time we apply a characteristic to divide a subject, we produce not only an array of co-ordinate divisions, but an equal number of chains of division subordinate to the subject.

Now we have seen that by finding some characteristic common to all members of a genus, but possessed by them in varying degrees or measures or in different ways, we can at one operation divide the genus into two or more co-ordinate species. We have seen, too, that further division of each of these species (each now to be considered as a genus) demands that we find a new characteristic possessed in varying degrees or measures or in different ways by all the members of it. The question now arises, which characteristic should we choose first for the primary division of the genus into species, and which should come second for the division of each species into sub-species? Allied to this is the question of what quality or qualities we can choose as the characteristic of division at each stage. Can we find any principles which will guide us in our choice?

CHAPTER IV

THE FUNDAMENTAL CONCEPTS WHICH UNDERLIE DIVISION

WHEN we consider each book separately, we are inclined to be overwhelmed by the multitude of qualities which go to make up the individual book. We saw very soon that books can be divided according to colour, size or author, but that these modes of division must be rejected in favour of subject. Subjects, too, offer a choice of qualities which we can use as characteristics for division; but, fortunately for the classifier, very few of these qualities need be taken into account because they are not incisive enough and would produce groupings unrelated to the way workers in the field approach their subject.

Ranganathan has devoted considerable time to the examination of the major universal schemes of classification with the object of discovering the principles, implicit as well as explicit, upon which they have been based.[1] He finds that all characteristics chosen (mostly quite intuitively) as the basis of division are related to those qualities which are the practical manifestations of five fundamental concepts. These are Time, Space, Energy, Matter and Personality. The first four of these are concepts basic to science, while the fifth is that quality which inheres in wholeness. Personality is that quality which underlies the infinite variety of things. Just as there are infinite varieties of colours, but only four primaries, so there are infinite varieties of subjects, but only five fundamental concepts. The recognition of this enables a classifier to take the infinitely variable quality (i.e. Personality) outside the bracket as it were and to manipulate the remaining constants with greater ease.

A very simple analogy is to be found in the field of mathematics where the personality of the objects manipulated is disregarded and pure numbers only form the basis of calculation. There is no such thing as two; to be two there must be

[1] Ranganathan. Fundamentals.

FUNDAMENTAL CONCEPTS WHICH UNDERLIE DIVISION

objects of some kind, but without the abstraction two there could only be the simplest of calculations. The very fact that we say 'two white mice' and not 'white mouse and white mouse' indicates that we are able, as it were, to de-personalise the phenomenon by removing the 'white mouse-ness' and leaving only the abstraction 'two'. We can state a general law about 'two':— $2 = 1 + 1$. This rule is valid whether applied to white mice, elephants or books, and yet if no-one had ever produced the abstraction 2, by de-personalising the phenomenon two white mice (or two somethings) we should be without a fundamental prop to civilisation. We should literally have to itemise each object in a collection when stating their numbers, thus:— white mouse and white mouse and white mouse. . . .

The significance of Ranganathan's fundamental concepts is that we can use a similar process of abstraction of a generalised rule in classification. Just as $1 + 1 = 2$ is a single concept, but has a myriad meanings when translated into terms of phenomena, so Matter, Energy, Space and Time are four concepts that acquire a myriad of meanings when translated into terms of phenomena by the meaning they acquire from the context of the subject to which they are applied.

Consider the subject *ploughing*. It is the name of an operation in agriculture. It represents the expenditure of energy in a certain way in the practice of agriculture. Let us put this statement out like a mathematical formula.

OPERATION OF PLOUGHING = AGRICULTURE + ENERGY

Now let us, as it were, factorise this statement: divide each side into its component parts:—

(Operation) of (Ploughing) = (Agriculture) + (Energy)

Now let us remove the factors on each side which identify the subject with Agriculture, and we get:—

Operation = Energy   (Equation 1)

which is a completely general concept, and unrelated to any particular subject.

Consider next the specific subject *rag-shredding in paper making*. This, set out as an equation gives us:—

OPERATION OF SHREDDING THE MATERIAL RAG = PAPER-
MAKING + ENERGY + MATTER

factorise:—
(Operation) of (Shredding) the (Material) (Rag) = (Paper-
                                    making) + (Energy) + (Matter)
remove the subject-identifying factors and we get:—

Operation + Material = Energy + Matter   (Equation 2)
We have already seen that Operation = Energy (equation 1): if we now subtract equation 1 from equation 2, side by side, we find that we get:—

Material = Matter

which gives us a second completely general concept.

Consider next the specific subject *history of England*. Set out, as in the above examples, it becomes:—
(History) of the (Geographic area) (England) = (History) in
                                        terms of (Space)
Remove the subject-identifying factors and we get:—

Geographic area = Space

It is easy to see that the concept Time could be abstracted in the same way.

We can test the working of the fundamental concepts for ourselves by going to the Decimal Classification, or any other scheme for that matter. The following list shows some of the places where these concepts can clearly be seen in use in the Decimal Classification.

TIME:—This is primarily used for the period divisions of history, but occurs as the third characteristic in dividing literature, and elsewhere throughout the scheme where chronological order proves useful: e.g., 271 Religious Orders.

SPACE:—This, too, is primarily associated with the history class, and manifests itself in that facet of history based on the geographical characteristic. Throughout the scheme we find ourselves directed to 'divide like 940–999' whenever the geographical region concerned is a valid approach to the subject. Incidentally, this is an intuitive recognition by the Decimal Classification that analysis of a subject into its facets is a powerful tool for other purposes than history.

ENERGY:—This is much less obvious in its manifestations. It usually presents itself as a problem to be solved, or a mode of work or approach. Indeed Ranganathan, in his Colon Classifi-

FUNDAMENTAL CONCEPTS WHICH UNDERLIE DIVISION

cation, usually calls the facet based on the characteristic Energy the *problem* facet. Medicine, (that is, the study of the human body or its parts) for instance, can be approached *via* anatomy, physiology or pathology, etc. It is possible to have anatomy of the eye, anatomy of the foot, physiology of the eye, physiology of the foot, pathology of the eye, pathology of the foot and so on. The study of the human body or its parts can be concentrated on one of a number of approaches or problems associated with the body or with one of its parts. It is these approaches or problems which the reader is asked to recognise as divisions of the Energy concept.

In a manufacture there is little difficulty because we know that actual physical energy is applied to material to produce the 'personalities.' In woodwork we recognise that planing, sawing, drilling, joining and so on involve energy; it is not difficult to appreciate that designing and overcoming faults also involve energy. The same is really true of the rather more involved manifestations in medicine. We can see, for example, the analogy to design in anatomy; to faults in disease.

In Education, energy is again represented by the problem facet—the problems here being those of teaching methods, curriculum building, and so on. The fabricative characteristic in engineering or manufacture, the operation facet in agriculture are both manifestations of energy. It requires a certain discipline to recognise the inner idea of energy behind the outward form of problem; but it can be done by studying the method of arrangement of the Decimal Classification, if allowance is made for its frequent lapses from observance of the rule that we should exhaust the potentialities of one characteristic before introducing another. Most Decimal Classification classes list energy divisions, even if nothing else. *See* 610, 658, etc.

MATTER:—This is another fairly simple concept to visualise in the forms it takes in various subjects. If we were classifying books on the manufacture of paper we should want some divisions based on the raw materials: these would relate to the concept Matter. The first characteristic of division for 691, building materials, is based on Matter.

PERSONALITY:—This is not really difficult to recognise if we bear in mind that the personality of a man is everything about him: that is, his wholeness. By extension of meaning, the term personality is used here for the wholeness of any subject. Personality inheres in the subject itself and gives colour to the other fundamental concepts transforming them into concrete things. For example:—1. It is the personality of the subject agriculture which transforms the general idea of energy into farming (i.e. crop-producing)—energy, which is the generalised name for all processes of farming. This personality derives from the crops which are the end-products of agriculture.

2. It is the personality of the subject medicine (i.e. study of the human body) which transforms the concept of energy into the body-studying-energy, which is a generalised name for all the branches of medicine.

3. It is the personality of the subject education (i.e. the transmission of knowledge) which transforms the concept of energy into knowledge-transferring-energy, which is a generalised name for all the problems of teaching, curriculum building, etc., that an educationist has to face.

Most subjects are divisible into parts or kinds, and about each of such parts or kind we can predicate the same things as about the whole subject. For example, we can not only have design of complete aeroplanes, but also design of fighter aircraft (kinds) and design of tail-planes (parts). These parts or kinds, therefore, are an integration of the other four concepts just as the whole is, and have a similar personality to the whole. That group of foci, or divisions, made up of these parts or kinds is called the personality facet of a subject. For example:—in aeronautics, the personality facet is in two parts: the one which is made up of the kinds of, and the other which is made up of the parts of, an aeroplane: in agriculture, the personality facet is that which is based on the kind of crop: we have kinds of religions and of languages. In each of these last three cases, the divisions which arise from there being kinds together constitute the personality facets of the three subjects cited.

All classificationists have great difficulty in finding unambiguous terms. For the sort of highly analytical classification which comes from the naming of characteristics, and from listing the divisions that result from them, the problem is even more difficult. Any terms used must denote a basic idea which is common to many subjects. We fail at first sight to recognise this common basic idea because the language of everyday speech has tended to fuse it and the special context into one word. We do not say 'male human' and 'female human', but 'man' and 'woman'. Similarly, in religion we do not say Christianity-sacred-book and Mahommedanism-sacred-book, but Bible and Koran. Many further examples can be found in the Colon Classification where the divisions listed under each facet are basic ideas and await fusion at the hands of the classifier.

If it is agreed, then, that the characteristics chosen as the basis of division can be related to these five fundamental concepts, it will be realised that we now have a series of abstractions which can be used, like numbers, without having to specify phenomena. That is to say, just as we can work in terms of numbers without referring them to kings, cabbages, or white mice, so we can work in terms of our fundamental concepts without reference to their meanings when translated into the world of specific subjects. We can, then, manipulate the order of subjects in a classification without knowing what the subjects actually are.

In Chapter II, we saw that the arrangement of books by subject should proceed from the general to the specific by the route: general—general treated specially—special treated generally—special treated specially. If this is to be achieved we must either do it by trial and error with the actual specific subjects themselves, which would be the work of a lifetime; or, we must find a principle which will enable us to do it mechanically. Let us begin with a concrete example of arrangement. Here are some imaginary works on aeronautical engineering.

1. The design of tail-planes in Britain in 1950.
2. Aeronautical design in Britain in 1940–49.
3. Aeronautical engineering in Britain in 1950.
4. Aeronautical engineering.
5. Tail-planes.
6. Design of tail-planes.
7. Aeronautical engineering in 1930–39.

48 FUNDAMENTALS OF LIBRARY CLASSIFICATION

All of these deal with the subject of aeronautical engineering in varying degrees of specificity. If we arrange them in the order considered most helpful in proceeding from the general to the specific, we shall get the following:—

Name of subject	Analysis in terms of fundamental concepts
Aeronautical engineering	The general subject as a whole.
Aeronautical engineering 1930–39	TIME specified.
Aeronautical engineering in Britain in 1950	SPACE and TIME specified.
Aeronautical design in Britain in 1950	ENERGY, SPACE and TIME specified.
Tail-planes	PERSONALITY (i.e. part of the whole sharing predicate).
Design of tail-planes	PERSONALITY and ENERGY specified.
Design of tail-planes in Britain in 1950	PERSONALITY, ENERGY, SPACE and TIME specified.

We can see from the right-hand column that in arranging in this order, we have divided by the least concrete of our fundamental concepts first, and used successive concepts in order of increasing concreteness. In other words, we arrange our specific subjects thus:—

1. Those divided according to time alone.
2. ,,   ,,   ,,   ,, space and time alone.
3. ,,   ,,   ,,   ,, energy, space and time.
4. ,,   ,,   ,,   ,, matter, energy, space and time.
5. ,,   ,,   ,,   ,, personality, matter, energy, space and time.

It is highly unlikely that the action of all the fundamental concepts will be apparent in the division of every subject. In agriculture, for example, the matter concept would manifest itself as the 'stuff of life', and the biochemical things which go to make growing crops; but since this is common to all agriculture, it need not be stated. Again, the space and time concepts are normally omitted from Agriculture (as from most subjects) unless specified, because all objective phenomena take place in the space-time continuum, and what is common may be omitted. This approach reveals that in most subjects space and time may be omitted from our calculations unless specified. Even though they are not specifically manifested in every subject, however, we must adhere to the order time, space, energy, matter and personality: that is, the order of increasing concreteness of ideas which culminates in personality.

We will again go to the Decimal Classification for an example of the working out of this order of characteristics, and consider class 362, Hospitals Asylums and allied (Welfare) societies, to which we shall, for convenience, refer as Welfare. This class is divided by the concepts personality (the beneficiaries without whom the subject would not exist) and energy (methods of applying relief), although the second is not often worked out in the schedules. In addition to this we may divide by the space concept (362·9 Special countries, divide like 940–999) and by the time concept, if we use the universal time divisions of Decimal Classification (table 2) for this purpose.

1. The general = 362 Welfare.
2. Treated from the viewpoint of time = 362·904 Welfare in the twentieth century.
3. Treated from the viewpoint of space and time = 362·942081 Welfare in Victorian Britain.
4. Treated from the viewpoint of energy = ? Institutional aid for all classes of the unfortunate. (N.B. no provision for this in Decimal Classification).
5. Treated from the viewpoint of personality = 362·52 Aid to the poor.
6. Treated from the viewpoint of personality and energy = 362·52 Workhouses.
7. Treated from the viewpoint of personality, energy, space and time = 362·520942081 Workhouses in Victorian Britain.

It will be noted that matter does not appear to come into the division of this class; but sufficient has been worked out to show

D

the relevance of the fundamental concepts. Unhappily, the Decimal Classification's notation mechanism does not allow the assembly of these subjects into the most helpful order. The order should be:—
Welfare: general.
Welfare in the 20th Century.
Welfare in Victorian Britain.
Methods of administering relief.
Aid to the poor.
Workhouses.
Workhouses in Victorian Britain.

The Decimal Classification, however, gives the following order :—
362 Welfare.
362·5 Aid to the poor.
362·52 Workhouses.
362·52094208I Workhouses in Victorian Britain.
362·904 Welfare in the 20th Century
362·94208I Welfare in Victorian Britain.

We can see from this that Decimal Classification's notation, its mechanism for preserving order, is not equal to the task of maintaining order among the subjects for which it makes provision. What is likely to be the fate, then, of subjects not yet listed, but which appear later? Failure of a notation in this respect is a serious fault.

Before we go any further, there is one point about the order of application or characteristics that must be cleared up. In order to arrange our subjects in increasing order of concreteness we must apply characteristics in the reverse order. A moment's thought shows us that this must be so.

When we perform the act of applying a characteristic, we really ask the question 'is the facet related to this characteristic specified in the subject or not?' The answer must obviously be yes or no. Let us consider come further examples in aeronautical engineering and proceed to ask the question of each specific subject. We shall indicate the characteristics, and hence the facets relating to them, by the initial letters P. M. E. S. T., we shall indicate 'yes' with X, and 'no' with O.

Specific Subject	Is facet specified?
	P. M. E. S. T.
1. Aeronautical engineering general	O O O O O
2. Aeronautical engineering 1930–1939	O O O O X
3. Aeronautical engineering in Britain in 1950	O O O X X
4. Aeronautical design in Britain in 1950	O O X X X
5. Design of aluminium aircraft in Britain in 1950	O X X X X
6. Designing aluminium tailplanes in Britain in 1950	X X X X X

We have actually applied the characteristics beginning with the most concrete and ending with the least concrete, yet the tabulation shows that the items listed fall into an order which begins with the least and ends with the most concrete. This happens because we arrange a series of digits or entries on the twin principles of *nothing precedes something* and *the lesser precedes the greater*. Ranganathan refers to this effect of reversal as the principle of inversion.

We must now turn our attention to the divisions we produce by applying a characteristic. Remember, when we divide up a genus into its species, we do so by using a characteristic which throws off two or more co-ordinate species at one step. Now these species must also be arranged in some order other than the accidental one in which they occur to us. They in their turn must contribute to our ideal of helpful order.

We have referred in Chapter II to the research done by Ranganathan in this matter. It must suffice here merely to repeat his findings. The series of co-ordinate species derived from a genus by application of a characteristic of division may be arranged in one of the following orders: 1. Canonical (i.e. complying with custom), 2. Evolutionary, 3. Spatial contiguity, 4. Chronological, 5. Alphabetical, 6. Increasing complexity, 7. Categorical.

Any one of these orders which proves to be the most useful for the particular array may be chosen, and must be mechanised by notation so that it shall be adhered to.

We have now arrived at this position: the order of application of characteristics is determined by the facet formula and the order of arrangement of co-ordinate classes is to be selected from the seven orders, and will be determined by the occasion.

What of the order of the subordinate species within any facet? For example, what will be the order of arrangement of the subordinate species within the problem facet of the class language? Let us look at 420, English language.

The co-ordinate classes in the problem facet are orthography, etymology, lexicology, synonyms, grammar, etc. The fifth of these, grammar, divides again into morphology, and syntax (still using the same characteristic) and syntax into arrangement of words, sentences, nouns, adjectives, etc. What is happening here? Each time we divide we move to subjects of smaller extension, so that we can say that the order of arrangement of subordinate species will be determined firstly by the order of application of the characteristics (those relating to time, for example, following those relating to space) and, within each focus of a facet will be in order of decreasing extension and, since each species becomes more definite in meaning than the genus from which it is derived, of increasing intension.

. . . . . .

It is essential that the principles treated in this chapter be properly assimilated, since they lay down the method upon which we feel any new schemes of classification ought to be based. While it is very unlikely that any librarian will be called upon to produce a new general scheme of classification, there is little doubt that many who work in research and similar libraries will be required to make schemes for the many special subjects inadequately treated by the existing general schemes. A rough and ready empirical scheme will absorb hours of unnecessary labour, both in the making and in the adjustment to changing conditions. The competent librarian must be able to make a good and effective scheme, and will be able to do so only if he has grasped the principles of division.

Such persons aside, the practice of classification and, incidentally, cataloguing (as we shall see in Chapter XI) will be greatly improved at all levels when these principles are absorbed. Technique will replace intuition.

CHAPTER V

PHASES AND PHASE ANALYSIS

IN Chapter III we have seen how a class of books may be broken down into groups by dividing them according to the manner or degree in which they possess a given attribute which we call the characteristic of division. Examples have been given which show that subjects can often be usefully divided according to any one of two or more different characteristics, and that, in fact, many a specific subject (or species) is abstracted from a more inclusive subject (or genus) by the application of successive characteristics. For example, *methods of hoeing potatoes* is abstracted from the class agriculture by the application of the characteristics 1. crop concerned and 2. process of cultivation.

When we look at the task of the classifier, which is to fit individual books into a scheme of classification according to their specific subjects, we find the analytical process of division again stands us in good stead. We note the successive characteristics of division used in our classification scheme for the subject concerned, and seek evidence of their operation in the subject of the book to hand. In most schemes the characteristics are not stated, but are implicit in the kinds of division enumerated. This makes the classifier's task more difficult, for he has first to learn to isolate the characteristic used by the maker of the scheme, and then to see how it operates in the book he is classifying.

Let us examine some specific subjects to see how we can discern the operation of characteristics of division in them. Woodworking, for example, may be divided in three quite distinct ways: by the kind of woodworking, as carpentry, cabinet making, fretwork etc. (Personality); by the material used, oak, ash etc. (Matter); and by the woodworking process (Energy). So we can set woodworking out with a brief statement of its facets thus:—

WOODWORKING	KIND (Personality)	MATERIAL (Matter)	PROCESS (Energy)
	Rough	Hardwoods	Designing
	Fine	Softwoods	Marking out
	Decorative	Laminated woods	Shaping Smoothing

The divisions within each facet will, of course, be focused much more sharply, as required. Each of the divisions under the second and third facets can (in theory) be predicated of each of the divisions under the first. Now consider the classifying of books dealing with each of the following subjects.

General woodworking. The specific subject is woodworking in general: all of the facets are present, yet none of them specifically: we can say that its focus in each is diffuse, and the subject is therefore unfaceted.

Woodworking joints. In this subject the facet *kind* is considered vacant because diffuse, and so, for the same reason, is the facet *material*. The subject is single-faceted.

Polishing oak cabinets. In this subject we can discern all three characteristics in action, as each of the facets is specified. The first is focused at *cabinet-making*, the second at *oak*, and the third at *polishing*. The subject is triple-faceted.

Each of the subjects given above finds its analysis in terms of *kind, material* or *process*, or a combination of them. We know, of course, that this is an over simplification: that the author of a book on one of these subjects may refer in the course of the book to art, science or history. But, like the physician who studies the symptoms of a man's malady but cannot isolate the malaise of spirit that goes with it, the classifier can diagnose the basic content of a book, even if his analysis misses its literary excellences. Each of the examples given above, then, falls completely within the conception of the class *woodworking*.

Here are some more specific subjects of a somewhat different nature:—

1. A dictionary of history.
2. Essays in biology.
3. A mathematical periodical.

These show the subjects history, biology and mathematics

treated in a quite general way: all of them are unfaceted, and yet each has something predicated of it. It is presented in the *form* of a dictionary, in the *form* of essays or in the *form* of a periodical. Indeed, we call these divisions the form divisions of these subjects. Their use indicates that we have ceased to divide by anything relating specially to history, biology or mathematics, and that we have entered a new phase of division: one relating wholly to the mode of presentation. Here the principles of division laid down in the last chapter do not apply: we require analysis of a cruder type. We can, indeed, say that we enter a different *phase* of division, one based on form.

The Decimal Classification indicates this phase change by the interposition of a zero between the part of the notation relating to the subject and the part relating to form. Bliss indicates it by changing his notation to arabic figures.

Here are some more specific subjects:—
1. Mathematics for the biologist.
2. Chemical analysis of the soil.
3. Effects of war on the birthrate.
4. Psychotherapy and the Christian doctrine of man.

One's first reaction to these is bewilderment, because they appear to be not one subject but two. They belong to classes of 'mixed' subjects, and classification schemes do not appear to provide for 'mixed main classes.' The classificationist has carefully separated the mathematical from the biological sciences in his scheme: he keeps chemistry with sciences and agriculture with useful arts. Yet here we have the mind of man, through its instruments books, bringing seemingly most incongruous bedfellows together. This problem is one of those which caused Jevons to declare that the classification of books is a logical absurdity.

A little thought, however, should show us that in each of the examples given above one of the two subjects thus thrown together is paramount. In the first, for instance, the real subject is mathematics, but it is treated with a *bias* towards biology (i.e. it deals with problems by using examples calculated to interest a biologist, and leaves out much of the mathematics which a biologist would not need). The second example shows the subject *chemical analysis* being used as a *tool* to study soils. In the third example we have the social effect of war on one aspect of genetics: it is a case of one subject *influencing* another. The last demands a closer acquaintance with the specific book before we can decide which subject the author has made paramount; but it is the *comparison* of one subject with another.

We have, then, three subjects which are obviously paramount and one which we shall see to be paramount when we can examine the book closely. We will assume that we have done this and that the paramount subject is religion. Then the subjects mathematics, agriculture, genetics and religion are the paramount subjects in the examples, and the subjects biology, chemical analysis, war and psychotherapy respectively are used to qualify these paramount subjects.

In none of these cases does the secondary subject represent a facet of the paramount subject. In every case the parts of these compound subjects would come from quite separate schedules of a general classification scheme. Indeed, in analysing these compound subjects we can be said to move over from one part of the scheme to another, and each of the subjects represents a separate phase of analysis. We can view what we have called the paramount subject as the first phase of the compound subject, and the secondary subject as the second phase. And, having called them by this name, we perceive at once the likeness to the change of mode of division when we entered the phase of dividing a subject according to its form of presentation.

We are now in a position to see that the specific subjects which go to make up a main class are not always completely described in terms of characteristics relating to the main class. On the contrary, they are often accretive, drawing to themselves parts of other main classes by way of relationships such as bias, use as a tool, influence and comparison. They may also be represented in special forms, such as dictionaries, essays and periodicals.

We will now state formally the conclusion to be drawn from this. When a specific subject consists of divisions drawn from the facets of a single main class, it is said to have only one phase. When a specific subject brings two sets of divisions drawn from two main classes into a relationship, it is said to have two phases. When a specific subject brings more than two such phases into a relationship, it is said to be multi- or poly-phased.

A few more examples may serve to make this point clearer. 'Teaching methods in elementary education' is a single-phased subject, because both of its foci (teaching methods, and children aged 5-11 years) are drawn from the facets of the same main class: i.e. education. 'Psychology for teachers' is a two-phased subject, because it is an assemblage of two areas of knowledge (psychology and education). 'Tomato-growing in greenhouses' is a single-phased subject because both its foci are drawn from the same main class: i.e. agriculture. 'Farming arithmetic' is a two-phased subject, because it is an assemblage of two areas of knowledge: i.e. agriculture and mathematics.

The examples so far given are very simple: the two phases shown have usually been simple unfaceted phases. We must remember, however, that the phase may be quite complex in its own make-up: each may consist of a subject with more than one facet. If, however, we proceed systematically according to the facet formula for each of the phases, we can break down every subject, no matter how complex, into its fundamental constituent parts. Take this imaginary subject, for instance:

'A statistical study of the use of X-rays for tracing faults in steel bearings.'

This divides into the following phases:—
1. Statistical study.
2. X-rays.
3. Faults in steel bearings.

Of these three phases, the third is obviously paramount, or the *primary* phase: the others will fall into their places as secondary or tertiary phases. Each of these phases, however, can be analysed by the principles of division. Statistical study, for example, is a subdivision, on a canonical (or conventional) basis, of mathematics.[1] X-rays is a subdivision, on the basis of wavelength, of the class physics; whilst the primary phase, faults in steel bearings, is a subdivision of the main class engin-

[1] Although D.C. places statistics as a division of Social science, reflecting but one use of the discipline.

eering made up of foci drawn from the commodity and problem facets (personality and energy) of that class. Later, this analytical method will be applied to the practical task of classifying books.

One thing we can clearly see is the difference between facets and phases. Facets are closely related to the subject: they are the successive layers of which a subject is built up, like the laminations in a piece of ply-wood. They are hard to prise apart. But phases are different: we can easily separate them one from another. They are loosely assembled.

Although we introduce the phases *via* the common subdivisions because these are easily seen as additions to a subject, there is really a difference between the form of presentation of a subject and the various types of phase relations. The use of form divisions is not a matter of assembly of two subjects but a way of presenting one. It has been described as 'dressing.'[1] A classifier working with a synthetic scheme of classification builds up each phase from the facets applicable to it: he joins the phases together with conjunctive signs representative of their functions, and he adds a symbol indicating the form of presentation.

It must be made clear that the idea of phase has been implicit in all modern schemes of classification for many years. Provision had been made for it to a certain extent in notation, and everything had been done except to give it a name. Ranganathan first gave the problem serious consideration, introduced the term phase for it and isolated a number of different kinds of phase such as bias, tool, influence and comparison.

The mathematical symbols of the Universal Decimal Classification, the zero, double-zero and treble-zero of the Decimal Classification, the systematic tables of Bliss: all these constitute an implicit recognition of the existence of phase. Often when a scheme allows us to divide a subject 'like the main classification', it is using phase as a mode of division.

Unfortunately in most schemes, owing to the failure to recognise the different kinds of phases, insufficient thought has been given to their representation in the notation, and to the method of assembling them. It is this that has contributed much to the breakdown of order in U.D.C. in the more minute areas

[1] Ranganathan. Classification and international documentation.

of knowledge. In the Decimal Classification, too, the double- and treble-zero is a clumsy and wasteful method of separating and identifying phases, and results in a very bad order. In point of fact, no scheme yet devised has produced a really good method of indicating phases.

There has been some small attempt at differentiation between some of the kinds of phases; but, again, it has been intuitive rather than rational. For example, U.D.C. uses a colon and a zero in brackets to show 'relation' and 'form' respectively. It is because phase was not fully understood at the inception of even the latest scheme that the allocation of symbols as indicators of the phases has been haphazard. We can call the symbols which are used to introduce phases the 'phase indicators', for obvious reasons. It is because no classificationist has yet produced a well-thought-out system of phase indicators that schemes fail to get the best out of phase-analysis.

So far, five kinds of phases have been isolated:—

1. Form phase (the method of presentation).[1]
2. Bias phase (one subject presented for the requirements of another).
3. Influencing phase (one subject influenced by another).
4. Comparison phase (one subject compared with another).
5. Tool phase (one subject used as a method of expounding another).

There may be others: [2]we wonder whether there should be an 'in regard to' phase, to express an idea such as 'American foreign policy in regard to U.S.S.R. in 1948'. Each phase should have its own indicator to make quite clear the basis upon which extra-facetal division is proceeding in a multi-phased subject.

In allocating such symbols, great care must be taken to see that they will ultimately arrange the material in the most useful order. That is to say, whether all phases are represented in a given group of subjects or not, they should fall into that order which puts the subsidiary phases into their proper relationships.

---

[1] Ranganathan has recently suggested that form should be part of the book number, not the class number.—Abgila, May 1950.

[2] During his visit to Britain (May 1950) Ranganathan mentioned his work on 'aspect' phase.

CHAPTER VI

NOTATION

So far, we have considered the arrangement of books and catalogues in the most helpful order. We have reached the conclusion that this order should be one of specific subjects arranged systematically and have stated a number of general principles about the nature of this order. We have mentioned specific subjects by name and talked by name of, for example, the main class Medicine, the main class History, and the main class Education. A moment's reflection will show that the names of these subjects or main classes do not indicate in any way the position which they are intended to occupy in the order of a scheme of classification.

It would be difficult to maintain a collection of books in systematic subject order according to a preconceived plan if the collection were not to be a museum piece. The order would be disturbed in use, and great difficulty might be experienced in replacing works in the order which had been hit upon as being the best. The more valuable the contents of the books and the nearer we had approximated to the most helpful order in their arrangement, the more they are likely to have been disturbed, because readers would have been finding what they wanted, and so removing books. It is pointless to go into the absurdities likely to arise from the necessity to reclassify each time a book is read and has to be replaced on the shelves. We should obviously indicate the subject of each book quite clearly somewhere on it, and, going further, we should give it some sort of mark or symbol to indicate where in the sequence it should be inserted. The symbol, of whatever kind, which is thus used to mechanise the process of sorting and replacement is known as the *notation*. We will therefore define this term before we go any further. Notation is a device for mechanising arrangement and must be composed of written symbols whose order is defined.

We can immediately think of two such sets of symbols:

arabic figures and the roman alphabet. There are others, however, and if we bear in mind the last clause of our definition we realise that if no suitable set of symbols exists, we can invent one so long as we are careful to define its order. A notation must consist of a series of digits which can be combined in a recognisable order. A digit can be defined as any numeral from 0–9, or any letter of the alphabet, or any single sign of a series used for constructing a notation. The digits of a notation do not require to possess a cardinal value: their only requirement is an ordinal value, and this can be assigned to them by their designer. This means, then, that not only are figures and letters at our disposal, but arbitrary signs as well, although for other reasons it may not be desirable to make use of them.

We have to bear in mind that many persons will have to understand the order expressed by the symbols chosen to mechanise the order of books, from the user of the library to the classifier himself. It is surely desirable that the chosen symbols should express order to the greatest number of people with the minimum of effort. This, of course, implies that the number of arbitrary signs should be kept as small as possible, and, if used at all, they should be restricted to the representation of phenomena of less frequent occurrence. In reality, therefore, we find that we are almost entirely confined to arabic numerals and roman letters.

There are other things which we require of a notation besides the ability to express order. We want to be able to say it easily when communicating it. The library user, when he reads it in a catalogue, must be able to commit it to memory easily for his brief passage to the shelf in search of his book. The reference assistant wants it to be easily written, for he will jot each symbol down countless times. The cataloguing and accessions departments will want it to be easily typed, for the typewriter enters largely into our economy.

Arbitrary symbols are difficult to say. Quite ordinary symbols may prove awkward to say if they are present in two varieties, even though we may distinguish them readily at sight. For example, BaCFd must be read as 'capital b, small a, capital cf, small d,' which is unrhythmic and clumsy.

Generally speaking, we can say that the shorter a notation, the easier it is to remember. This is not entirely so, however. Other factors which enter into ease of remembrance are the kinds of symbols used, the way in which they are grouped, and associations which may be inferred from any of the symbols (i.e. their mnemonic value).

The use of the typewriter restricts the number of species of symbols available to some extent, for although special keys can be fitted to typewriters the number of keys which can be so changed is strictly limited on the normal keyboard: this may not always be so, in view of the experiments now going on with variable type faces. Some symbols of different species have the same or a very similar shape, and their use can lead to confusion: an obvious example of this lies in the likeness of the letter O to the zero. Indeed, a typist often uses the same key for both.

We can summarise briefly by saying that it is desirable for a notation to be easy to read, write, type, say and remember.

It is also very desirable that a notation should be brief. After all, it often has to go on the spine of a book, which is not always very wide. It has, too, to be written in a good many records, and the shorter the notation the quicker the operation of writing. Brevity in a notation must not, however, be bought at the cost of order.

The fact must be faced that the higher the degree of intension of a class, the longer will be its notation. Classification demands the representation of an infinite series of subjects by a finite series of symbols. It is obvious that in the remoter orders of intension notation must be long. It is possible to have a short notation only by sacrificing co-extensiveness with the subject of the book. Bliss, confronted with this problem, has decided not to seek co-extensiveness where this leads to long notation. This, however, is not a solution of the problem, though his pleasantly short symbols lead us to hope that it is. Ranganathan has stated that he prefers to seek co-extensiveness, even if it means a very long symbol. Such a symbol, he claims, always remains as a challenge to the classificationist, urging him to seek further and more incisive methods of representing subjects in notation. Even the longest notation can be made to seem less so by the provision of occasional 'pauses', which break the symbols into groups of digits.

Having decided some of the more obvious requirements of a notation, let us examine the materials from which we can fashion it. Each separate symbol of any series we shall refer to as a *digit*, whether it be numerical, alphabetical or an arbitrary sign. Each group of the same kind of symbol we shall call a *species* of symbols. Let us examine each species in turn.

Numerals divide (in the western world) into two species: arabic and roman. Arabic numerals are very easily manipulated for all purposes; but roman numerals are very rigid, not permitting decimal division, for instance, and, being compounded of letters, would confuse in practice with the roman alphabet in a notation which attempted to combine the two.

Letters have a large number of species, based on function, design or origin. There are, among others, the roman, italic and greek alphabets, all divisible into upper and lower case. These give us six species, each of which can, in turn, be accented, overlined or underlined to distinguish further species if necessary.

Arbitrary signs have in theory, an infinite number of species. In point of fact, however, the only practicable ones are punctuation marks (some of which have a degree of recognised order) and mathematical signs (whose order has never become fixed). The former have been used by Bliss, the latter by the Universal Decimal Classification.

In making use of any of these various kinds of symbols, we may decide to limit ourselves to one species only, numbers or letters. If we do so, we are said to use a pure notation. If we use more than one species of symbol to represent subjects, numbers and letters, we are said to use a mixed notation. There was a time when a pure notation was considered to be preferable to a mixed one, but this view has lost favour in face of the growing tendency in all schemes to use more than one species of symbol. The Decimal Classification, the classic exponent of purity in notation, succumbed to this tendency in its 13th edition, and provided for the permissive use of letters as phase introducers: for example, d—language, f—form, k—time, p—place, etc.

All classificationists have used symbols somewhat arbitrarily in making their schemes, without apparently considering their fitness for their respective functions. There is need for an examination of the relation between species of symbols and the elements of a classification scheme they are required to represent. Out of such an examination a more economical use of notation might be devised. As examples for the use of different species for different elements we can cite the modern accepted practice of all schemes of representing main classes by upper case roman letters, of Bliss's use of arabic numerals for common subdivisions, and of Ranganathan's use of lower case roman letters for the same function.

Looking back to the previous chapters, we find that we were able to isolate three different elements in a subject. First, there is the main class in which it is contained: then there are the facets of that class which give a subject its own specificity, and, thirdly, in some cases there are two phases or more. It is desirable that each of these elements should be represented in a notation, and the more exactly this is done the more exactly shall we be able to state a subject in terms of notation.

The Decimal Classification indicates main classes by the numerals 0–9 and so does U.D.C.. Subject Classification, Congress, Bliss and Colon all prefer to indicate main classes with roman capitals. When we move on to the facets of each class, and examine the above schemes to see what they use to enumerate the divisions, we find Decimal Classification, U.D.C. Subject, Congress* and Colon all using arabic numerals, and only Bliss using roman capitals. Turning next to phases, we find that Decimal Classification, U.D.C., and the Subject Classification always use arabic numerals, whilst Colon and Bliss use either letters or figures, according to the tables from which the notation is drawn.

One thing we do notice is that the Decimal Classification sometimes announces its change of phase: for example, 09 says very effectively, 'We will now divide geographically,' 0001 says 'What went before considered in relation to what follows,' 00

* This is not strictly true of Congress, which uses a second roman capital for enumerating divisions before introducing arabic numerals.

says 'From the viewpoint of,' and o says 'In the form of.' The same thing crops up in the Subject Classification, which uses a full stop to indicate that what follows is a categorical number. Colon shows the form phase by the use of lower case letters, Bliss by the use of arabic numbers. When a symbol is used to announce a change of method of division, it can be called an *indicator digit* because it indicates a new method of division. The zero in the Decimal Classification is always used as an indicator digit, sometimes for a phase indicator (as when it brings in common subdivisions) and sometimes for a facet indicator (as when it brings in the chronological divisions in history).

Now, since we are really very restricted in the species of symbols we can use, we ought to get as much out of them as possible.

It ought to be decided before the next scheme of classification is made what are the essential elements, and how they can be represented by what we have in the way of notational raw material. A clue is given to us by the 000, 00, and 0 of the Decimal Classification. We never mistake a 5 which follows the first of these for a 5 which follows the second or third. The phase indicator has, as it were, coloured the numbers which follow it, so that they take on a different meaning in each case.

This principle could be followed for other purposes: facets could be indicated by digits which would colour the symbols which followed to give them a peculiar meaning, just as in the Decimal Classification the zero after 942 gives the numbers that follow a chronological meaning. The same sort of effect could be obtained with a less expenditure of digits by breaking the longer species of symbols into groups and relating each group to a facet. For example, the alphabet (omitting the letters O and I, can give us three groups of eight digits each, which can be apportioned to the first three facets of any subject, that is, those related to personality, matter and energy.

To summarise our remarks on the sort of notation which any future scheme of classification should have if it is to do its work economically, we may say: it needs to be able to enumerate distinctively the main classes and allow for the growth of new

E

ones; it needs to differentiate between the facets of any class, either by an apportionment of symbols or by facet indicators; it needs to be able to indicate phase changes and to show which phase is being used. All this points to at least three and possibly four species of notation.

One important aspect of notation remains to be considered, namely, flexibility. It is felt that this is so important that the next chapter has been devoted to it.

CHAPTER VII

NOTATIONAL FLEXIBILITY

It must not be supposed that notation is a by-product of subject classification. It had been used in many libraries, classified and unclassified, long before Dewey invented his Decimal Classification.

In its simplest form it consisted in relating the books to the bookcase and shelf in which they were situated. Suppose bookcases were lettered A–Z, and the shelves within each were numbered 1–30, then a book with the symbol G 25 on its back would belong to the 25th shelf of case G. By adding a further letter or number even the position of the individual book on a particular shelf could be indicated.

If we were never to add any more books to a collection, this method could be used even in a classified library. It is possible to combine helpful order and fixed location quite happily. Add a few books, however, and the shelf position of many other books is changed, involving much alteration of numbers. Add more books, and others have to be moved to different shelves, so that shelf numbers have to be altered. Add enough books, and even the case numbers have to be altered.

Since a library is almost without exception a growing organism, it is obvious that fixed location would impose a heavy burden of renumbering and stock movement on the staff of a library. The aim of all library technique is to reduce drudgery to the minimum so as to release staff for the higher task of personal service to the readers, so that a method of applying notation which is more efficient than fixed location is essential. Dewey's solution to this is the decimal system and relative location.

Here the principle is to ignore the position of the books in relation to the shelves, but to relate the notation to the subjects of the books. It then does not matter how many books on gardening we add, since they all take the same symbol and are automatically fixed in their place with the other books on gardening. Having once given all our subjects a symbol which fixes their order, we can give a symbol to additions in any subject group without disturbing the order. We could, for example, number all our subjects from 1 to 50,000, or however many we have—and we should have provided for the addition of an indefinite number of books to any of these subjects, so that they would all fall into their proper places.

But we have seen that knowledge is ever-growing: that no matter how careful we may be, we cannot even enumerate all existing subjects, while future subjects are beyond our reach. How are we to allow for the subjects which we have omitted from our schedule, or for the new ones which arise after we have drawn it up? We could, of course, leave gaps in our numbers, using intelligent anticipation as to future requirement. This was done by Brown and by the makers of the Library of Congress scheme. Both of them used what is known as an integer notation, that is, a notation which runs 1, 2, 3 ... 9, 10, 11 ... 19, 20, 21, and so on. The trouble about such a notation is that no matter how intelligent our anticipation might have been, sooner or later it fails us, and we find ourselves faced with a new subject which demands to be inserted between two others bearing consecutive numbers. The use of an integer notation with gaps for future expansion is only a postponement of the problem of meeting the expansion of a library. Some other more permanent solution must be found: we must find a series of symbols which will grow with our growing demands on them.

A partial solution can be found in the use of numbers read as a decimal fraction. If we number a group of subjects from 1 to 9, and then find that between 7 and 8 a new subject crops up, we can add a digit to 7 and bring in the numbers 71 to 79 (to be read as seven-one to seven-nine, NOT seventy-one to seventy-nine). This immediately gives us a further nine symbols with which to number new subjects.

If we have only one sort of order to preserve, this will be fairly adequate for our needs. If all the new subjects which come to us for insertion into our order prove to be subdivisions of subjects for which we have already provided symbols, all

NOTATIONAL FLEXIBILITY

will be well. Suppose we have the number 6359 for floriculture: if a book on the subject of rose culture comes along we can give it the number 63591, and this, read as a decimal fraction, brings rose culture immediately next to the books on flower culture. This is a decided improvement on integer notation.

Decimal implies division into ten parts; but, in fact, we only accommodate nine subdivisions: the zero is 'understood' in the number which indicates the general heading. Unfortunately, although this sytem of notation has been used by Dewey in his Decimal Classification and much praised for its infinite expansibility, it fails to take note of the fact there there are two ways in which new subjects can come to us. One is by the appearance of subjects subordinate to existing subjects, as shown in the example just given; but the other is by the appearance of new subjects co-ordinate in rank with existing subjects. Earlier on, when dealing with building, we showed how the new trade of electrical wiring has introduced a new subject co-ordinate with bricklaying and plastering into the sphere of the subject building during the last hundred years. This is not the last time such a thing will happen, and a classification scheme which is to have any degree of permanence must make allowances for this to happen at any point. Let us make a diagram:—

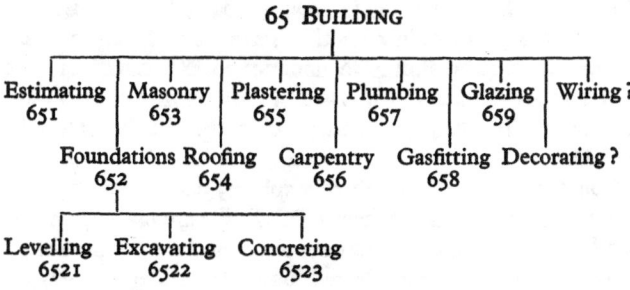

From this, we can see at once that decimal numbers are able to cope with the expansion by subordinates as under 652, but there are no numbers left after glazing 659 to accommodate co-ordinate subjects like decorating, wiring, or any other subjects which might arise. The decimal notation proves to be

70 FUNDAMENTALS OF LIBRARY CLASSIFICATION

hospitable to increase in chain, but not in array. We could, of course, give decorating the number 6591, and wiring 6592; but, although this would solve the immediate problem, it would create another if ever we wished to subdivide the subject glazing, because the decimal divisions of its symbol would already have been used. What we want is a notation which can meet expansion due to new co-ordinate as well as new subordinate subjects: one which will offer hospitality in array as well as chain.

We require some device for continuing to add successive co-ordinate numbers beyond nine without indicating subordination. We can get this effect by adding accents: for example, 1, 2, 3 ... 8, 9, 1̇, 2̇, 3̇ ... 8̇, 9̇, 1̈, 2̈, 3̈ ... 8̈, 9̈; or by underlining and overlining the digits; or, by using a letter of the alphabet as a repeater, for example 1, 2, 3, 4, ... 1a, 2a, 3a, 4a, etc. Ranganathan has adopted a method of doing this without using a different species of symbol. He chooses one of the series of digits ordinarily in use to be the repeater. He limits himself to the first eight decimal subdivisions of any number, and reserves the ninth as the repeater, beginning then at 1 again. His numerals will thus read: 1, 2, 3, 4, 5, 6, 7, 8, 91, 92, 93, 94, 95, 96, 97, 98, 991, 992, 993, etc.

It may seem at first sight that confusion is likely to arise; but, in fact, once the convention is grasped that 9 is never used by itself, but only to introduce another series of eight co-ordinate numbers, it is quite simple to understand. Ranganathan calls this the octave device, and it was first used by him in his Colon classification. In 1948 it was adopted by the F.I.D. for use in the U.D.C.

Though unconventional in this sphere, octave device has a perfect analogy in music, where ABCDEFG are used again and again for series of notes of varying pitch, and are distinguished by such words as top, middle and lower. In octave notation we can have a similar list of thirty-two co-ordinate subjects (that is, subjects of equal rank derived from a major inclusive subject by the consistent application of a characteristic) ranging from 1 to 9998, and the 9, 99, and 999 can be regarded as another way of saying 'top,' 'middle' and 'lower.'

By the use of these two techniques, decimal notation and the octave device, we can meet demands for expansion in knowledge, whether they come as a result of new subjects stemming off from those we have already recognised, or as a result of the appearance of new subjects equal in rank to those in any part of our schedule. Looking at our diagram above, we can say that it presents an array of subjects reading from left to right, and a chain of subjects reading downwards. The techniques of decimal notation and octave device (or one of the other methods of securing the same effect) give us infinite hospitality in chain and array.

Throughout this explanation we have postulated the appearance of new subjects to necessitate these techniques. In point of fact it requires little imagination to foresee new subordinate subjects, but just because new co-ordinate subjects are almost impossible to foresee (otherwise we should have listed them) the need for the octave device tends to be minimised, or even overlooked. There are many major subjects whose divisions are already too numerous to fit into the series 1 to 9, however, and the use of the octave device can be seen to be valuable here, without the postulation of further co-ordinate divisions.

So far, our discussion of notational flexibility has proceeded as though numbers were the only symbols available for our use. But we must remember the definition which occurred early in Chapter VI: notation is a device for mechanising arrangement and must be composed of written symbols whose order of arrangement is defined, and the subsequent statement that letters of the alphabet constitute one such series of symbols. The alphabet has one immediate advantage: the letters composing it have no cardinal value, so we have no habitual attitude towards them to discard.

As Bliss observes, letters can give us a series of up to 26 co-ordinate divisions at one step. We have seen, however, that it may be wiser to count on using the consonants only. This puts 21 symbols at our disposal. If we select one of these to be our repeater, we can have a series of 40 co-ordinate symbols at our disposal with the use of a maximum of two digits. An alphabetical notation can, therefore, be just as hospitable in chain and array as one composed of numbers, whilst, owing to its wider base (20 digits as opposed to 8), it is more economical in its use of digits.

Arbitrary symbols, too, can be given similar powers once their order has been defined, but it seems inadvisable to use them, except for the most advanced work, as their employment demands a large measure of intellectual co-operation from the users of the scheme, and this is only forthcoming from those who recognise the need for such a discipline to secure advances in any sphere of activity. That specialists are willing to make the effort to grasp necessary disciplines, is shown, for example, by the electronic engineer's use of greek letters to indicate phenomena in his own field.

We have arrived, then, at the point where we can realise the need for two-way expansion in notation, and have seen how this need can be met quite comfortably. But there is yet another factor which must be considered.

When discussing helpful order we saw how we could divide a subject first according to one characteristic and then according to another. Now we have had to admit the impossibility of enumerating all known and possible subjects which arise from the division of a major subject according to one characteristic: how much more impossible will it be, then, to enumerate all the known and possible subjects arising from division by two or even more successive characteristics. All that has been said so far about hospitality has been based upon the assumption that only one characteristic is used as the basis of division.

Fortunately the representation of the subjects arising from the use of successive characteristics does not involve us in the necessity for further notational tricks. All that we need is some sort of separating device to keep the symbols relating to one characteristic apart from those relating to another. Dewey has found it desirable to do this in the history class, where divisions based on the characteristic chronology are separated from those based on the characteristic geography by a zero, thus allowing infinite subdivision of the subject from both aspects. The zero is also used as a separating device when form is used as a method of division, and permits continued subject subdivision simultaneously:—

503 Scientific periodicals.
510·3 Periodicals in mathematics.
511·03 Periodicals in arithmetic.

This separating device is such a potent one that it ought to be used to give classification a higher degree of flexibility than is found in any of the enumerative schemes. It should be used to mark off the change of characteristic whenever it occurs.

Dewey, however, did not use this principle save occasionally and almost by accident. Ranganathan developed it by using a colon to separate one facet from another. But it did not need to be a colon. We could get the same effect with an oblique stroke, or a dash, or, in fact, any symbol quite distinct from those used to enumerate divisions. A notation which thus takes cognisance of change of characteristic, and separates the various facets of subjects is called a *faceted notation*. This is how it appears in use:—

$$L4:42$$

i.e. L (medicine) 4 (respiratory system) :42 (infectious diseases) which means medicine divided first by the organ concerned and then by the problem involved.

A faceted notation, then, allows us to mechanise the order of the facets, indeed, to show where we change the characteristic used for division. In the example just given, L4:42, we are writing in a sort of code the following message:—

'The books in this section deal with medicine, subdivided first by the organ concerned, which in this case is the respiratory system, and then (colon) by the problem concerned, which is pathology of a special nature, in this case infectious diseases.'

Faceted notation does more than this, however. It will be remembered that we agreed that we should arrange our material thus:—1. the general treated generally, 2. the general treated specially, 3. the special treated generally, 4. the special treated specially. Now if a classificationist could enumerate all subjects, past present and future, he could list them in this order and all would be well. We know, however, that he cannot do this. Every scheme once printed is at the mercy of its users wherever any part of the exercise of its functions is left uncoded. The means of fixing the preferred order lies in the mechanising device, or as we call it, the notation. This, therefore, should be such as to preserve the preferred order no matter what growths in knowledge, demanding expansion of the classification schedules, may occur. This the faceted notation can do, by the very mode of its construction.

Let us take the example used above, L4:42 (infectious diseases of the respirato y organs). We find ourselves with two facets, each represented in the notation:—

L	4	:	42
Medicine	Respiratory organs		Infectious diseases

Medicine is the general subject, and if it is treated generally, it will refer to no organ and no problem. These facets are, therefore, vacant and the classmark is merely L:. Respiratory organs is a special part of the subject of medicine, but a book on this subject could deal with their anatomy, physiology, pathology, etc., in fact, be a quite general book on a rather special subject. Although it would have one facet specified, the problem facet would be vacant, and we should therefore get the class mark L4:. If we add infectious diseases to this subject, it becomes more specialised: we are treating the special specially, both facets are specified, and we arrive at the class mark we began with.

Now let us assemble the subjects without all the explanation:—

L: —Medicine (general treated generally).
L:42 —Infectious diseases (general treated specially).
L4:   —Respiratory organs (special treated generally).
L4:42—Infectious diseases of respiratory organs (special treated specially).

We can see at once that a faceted notation of this kind, provided the separating device ranks before the digits used to enumerate divisions, automatically sorts subjects into their proper order. We must, of course, have the facets in the correct order to begin with.

In the Colon Classification from which these examples of faceted notation are drawn, it is a rule that when a colon is not followed by any further digits, it shall be omitted. The symbols in the above list should, therefore, read:—

L
L:42
L4
L4:42

CHAPTER VIII

MNEMONICS AND AUTONOMY FOR THE CLASSIFIER

IN preceding chapters we have noted that knowledge is constantly increasing and that new subjects are always arising. It has been shown that a scheme of classification must be able to expand in order to meet the demands of growing knowledge. We have seen how mechanisms for maintaining order (i.e. notation) have had to be thought out so that they would reflect the fluidity of the schedules of classification schemes, which themselves are reflections of changing ideas.

How, then, does a scheme of classification proceed to accommodate new subjects? Generally the method is for the maker of the scheme himself, or the editorial board which is the self-perpetuating substitute for an immortal classificationist, to undertake periodical revisions of the scheme, taking the opportunity of bringing it up-to-date as regards new subjects which have appeared since the previous edition. Needless to say, this is a slow process, and must of necessity lag a long way behind progress of knowledge: particularly in the sciences and technology where every day brings its advances. Some device is needed for the transfer of this power of revision, or as much of it as is feasible, from the centre to the periphery: from the classificationist to the classifier.

To see how this might be achieved, let us look at existing schemes in the hope of finding some indications of efforts made to give autonomy to classifiers.

Probably the first thing we notice about all modern schemes is the provision of what Decimal Classification calls common subdivisions: that is, a series of subdivisions based on form of presentation, which have been given constant symbols. In the Decimal Classification they consist of the numbers 1 to 9 and their subdivisions, which may be added after a zero to the notation for any subject. Their value is constant: for example, 03 is always dictionaries, 04 always essays and so on. Bliss achieves the same effect with his anterior divisions, represented, again, by numbers having a constant value. Brown mixes his form divisions in with his categorical numbers, but the principle is the same, as it is with Colon which uses lower case italics. Congress alone lacks this device; but as it was originally intended only for internal use, the scheme did not demand autonomy for the classifier. For it is just this that these common subdivisions give in a limited degree: autonomy for the classifier.

Another way in which the classifier is given, as it were, the 'freedom of the scheme' is in the provision of a table of geographical divisions for application wherever they would be useful. Decimal Classification does this. These divisions may either be used in specially noted places, where it is directed to 'divide like 940-999', or wherever geographical division would be useful, provided it is introduced by 09. Bliss, too, provides this facility; but gives more than one set of tables, each to be used for a limited and carefully prescribed purpose. Brown and Colon each provide for geographical division, where such is desirable, by means of tables of symbols having constant values. Again, Congress does not provide any such tables for universal application.

Here we will pause to note an important fact about enumerative schemes: not only is it impossible for them to show any future subjects, but they cannot even hope to tabulate all existing ones that are known to the classifier at the time of writing. In the case of classes where the space facet is not normally expressed for example, most schemes, as we have seen, are content to list the subjects resulting from the personality and energy facets, leaving the space facet implicit, and providing the apparatus for constructing a suitable notation for it. One of the reasons for the greater bulk of the Library of Congress schedules is that they attempt to enumerate all subjects without resorting to ' tables of constants.'

Decimal Classification provides a number of other instances of devolution. There are the linguistic numbers which are used in dividing literature and non-Christian religions, as well as philology. Occasionally one part of the scheme uses the divisions printed for another: for example, at 635·933 species of flowers, a section of floriculture, it is directed to divide like 583-9, the personality divisions of botany. Frequently, too, it is directed to 'divide like the main classification'. In Colon Classification, such devices are more freely used with the object of heightening the power of the classifier: indeed, the divisions of one class are frequently employed in other classes where their use is valid.

All these are very practical and quite mechanical methods for transferring to the classifier some of the functions of the maker of the scheme. They all help, in some degree, to keep a scheme of classification abreast of the times. Such devices, because they use symbols in such a way that their meaning is constant and thus tends easily to be committed to memory, are known as mnemonics, thus gaining a name based on a quite secondary attribute. Mnemonics which thus rely on lists of divisions, tables or parts of schedules are called by Ranganathan scheduled mnemonics.

Such scheduled mnemonics do not, however, assist the classifier who is confronted with an article or a book on a quite new subject. Suppose a book on atomic engineering appears: how are we to classify it pending the arrival of a new edition of the scheme of classification we use, or a decision from the editorial board in answer to our request for help?

Earlier we suggested that if the maker of a scheme named the characteristic he used for division at any point, it would aid those who would later follow in his footsteps. Suppose, for example, Dewey had told us that 621 mechanical engineering, must be divided first by motive power; we should know that atomic engineering would have to be a subdivision of 621 co-ordinate with steam, hydraulic and heat engineering. But we could not be certain of choosing the right number: that is to say, the number Dewey himself would have chosen. Is there any way of assisting the classifier to choose the number the classificationist would have chosen if the subject had been in existence when he first drew up the schedules? Ranganathan's suggestions on page 129 of his Prolegomena offer interesting possibilities in this direction.

The divisions within each facet of a scheme are enumerated, as we have seen, by a series of digits. It is possible to allocate to each of these digits a certain group of associated ideas (somewhat after the manner of Roget's *Thesaurus*). When a classifier is confronted with a quite new subject, he first reduces it to its fundamental constituents, thus:—

(Atomic) (Engineering)

and so isolates the particular constituent which is new. This constituent will not appear in the list of divisions of the appropriate facet. A place has to be found for it, however, and preferably a place which will not offend against the helpful order already existing.

The classifier, therefore, turns to the list of digits with the group of associated ideas set out under each, and proceeds to 'match up' the newly-discovered focus with one of the ideas in the groups. When he finds a corresponding idea, he uses the digit which indicates it to enumerate the new division.[1]

As an example, let us imagine that we have to classify a periodical article on faults in plastic containers. Let us assume that the class number for plastic containers is MX4/5, the oblique stroke being used to separate facets. We know that 'faults' is a problem, and that it must fall somewhere within the energy facet which comes next. In order that the number which we choose shall be correct, we must not choose at random but consult the groups of associated ideas to find one which we can relate to 'faults.' The 'pathology' group expresses the idea of something being wrong. Pathology is in the group of ideas numbered 4, so we take this digit to represent faults in the energy facet of the subject. We add 4 to the symbol for plastic containers, taking care to precede it by the separating device, and so get the complete class-mark MX4/5/4. We can be reasonably confident that the maker of the scheme would have done the same. He would probably take it to the second octave (i.e. 94) because it is one of the problems that arise after the completion of manufacture.

[1] At the time of writing (June 1950) Ranganathan is engaged on research into the full possibilities of this idea to which he has provisionally given the name 'primordial schedules'.

In the Colon Classification, Ranganathan only brought this idea to the level of consciousness after having first made his schedules, as a result of wondering just why he chose *this* number instead of *that*. His division enumerators, therefore, do not always fit in with his unscheduled mnemonics. A future 'ideal' scheme, however, should take cognisance of this device from the outset, and only allocate digits in accordance with the list of basic ideas.

As a matter of fact, the digit 4 is actually the number used by Ranganathan to denote a condition of wrongness, along with other associated ideas, and it has come to mean that to us also, owing to our frequent use of it in classificatory experiments.

The following are a few of Ranganathan's basic ideas, together with their associated digits.

4—Pathology, disease, transport, interlinking, synthesis, etc.
5—Aesthetics, emotion, women, water, liquid, ocean, foreign lands, aliens, external environment, not intrinsically sound, crime, etc.
6—Finance, money, mysticism, abnormality, phylogeny, evolution, etc.
7—Accounts, value, personality, ontogeny, etc.

The associations contained in these lists are very noticeably personal ones: note the association of feminine ideas with instability! It should be possible for such lists to be drawn up on completely rational principles, in which personal predilection would play little part.

These associations were called by Ranganathan 'unscheduled mnemonics,' this rather negative name being given merely to distinguish them from the simpler and more widely-used variety which is derived from lists or tables in the schedules of a scheme. We felt that a more positive name would be more suitable for what promises to be a valuable tool in any future scheme of classification. 'Seminal mnemonics' seems more suggestive of their true nature.

If subjects can be broken down into their fundamental constituents, and these constituents can be related to one of the digits used as division enumerators, then classification has moved a long way towards becoming an artificial language of ordinal symbols. What such a language demands is a grammar and syntax, which can be supplied from examination of other schemes. Classification can then move on from its position in the extreme rearguard of knowledge, and become an essential aid to science and other information services.

CHAPTER IX

THE FACET FORMULA IN AN ENUMERATIVE CLASSIFICATION

WE have been considering the desiderata of a thoroughly efficient scheme of classification, and have found that the schemes we have in daily use only partly measure up to the standards we have set. For instance, none of them is faceted except occasionally and almost by accident, none of them offers infinite hospitality in chain and array, and in none of them does the system of division appear to be consciously based on any coherent body of principle. However, because the order of every scheme, if its object is to achieve maximum usefulness, will be approximately the same, the principles to be inferred from the surface manifestations of all schemes must be fundamentally the same. If the theory which we have set out to expound in this book is correct then, in so far as the schemes obey such principles they function efficiently, and where they neglect them they fail to give satisfaction (cf. the unhelpful hotchpotch in Decimal Classification at 629·1, 629·2; 338, 320, and many other places where these principles are flouted).

Facet analysis, we have tried to show, is the bedrock of efficient classification. It is the conscious approach to what is otherwise subconscious and often hidden in an enumerative scheme of classification. We shall see that this is so if we can observe the pattern resulting from facet analysis in an enumerative scheme. Let us, then, take the Decimal Classification and, with the facet formula as our tool, see if we can prise apart the schedules to discover, firstly, if division in this scheme is based on the fundamental concepts, and, secondly, if the scheme observes the order of application of characteristics which will result in an arrangement of subjects in an order of increasing concreteness.

Let us begin with the concept Time. Throughout the schedules of the Decimal Classification we are permitted to divide any subject according to time, if we introduce it by the digits 09. For example:—

630·904 Agriculture in the 20th century.
709·02 Art in the middle ages.

From this we can see that provision is made for the representation of the time facet. By the same device, the space facet can also be introduced (divisions are drawn from the history schedules). The application of this useful device throughout the scheme was in the nature of an afterthought in the construction of the Decimal Classification, and it has had to be included with the common subdivisions as though space and time were forms rather than facets. It was an instinctive employment of the space and time facets, without a full realisation that space and time are essential parts of all subjects, though not always specified. The following are examples of division according to the space concept:—

630·942 Agriculture in England.
709·4 Art in Europe.

The next facet for which provision must be found is that corresponding to energy (proceeding in order of increasing concreteness). In classes 630, 629·1, 629·2, and 658 divisions will be found under each, set out as follows:

630 AGRICULTURE	629·1 AERO ENGINEERING
631 Operations	629·13 Aeronautics
632 Hindrances and protection	
	629·132 Aerostatics
	629·133 Aerodynamics
	629·134 Meteorological conditions
	629·135 Navigation
629·2 AUTO ENGINEERING	658 INDUSTRIAL MANAGEMENT
629·23 Construction (under which are also wrongly subsumed materials and parts)	658·1 Promotion and financing
	658·2 Plant management
629·233 Testing	658·3 Personnel management

84   FUNDAMENTALS OF LIBRARY CLASSIFICATION

629·234 Manufacture opera-   658·5 Shop management
tions

658·7 Buying, warehousing

658·8 Selling

These deal with the challenge to man's mind made by the subjects, and man's response to them: they are what we call problems. Just as one learned in an early grammar lesson that a verb is a 'doing' word, so we may say that in classification the energy facet is the 'doing' facet. We can see that the Decimal Classification provides energy facets if the subject calls for them.

Facets based on matter are not so common. In abstract subjects they will obviously not appear at all. In quite a number of concrete subjects, also, matter is unspecified (for example, 610 and 630). Nevertheless, in certain subjects it must be specified because the raw material from which the personality of the end products must be shaped is specified in the literature of these subjects. In these cases, suitable divisions will usually be found in the Decimal Classification. For example:

629·1342 Aircraft materials
691   Building materials

Finally we come to personality, a term which we have had the greatest difficulty in defining, but which we have said denotes 'the thing itself.' We will attempt a final clarification of its meaning by analogy and example, before proceeding to look in the Decimal Classification for the divisions based upon it. It is possible to define most specific subjects in terms of a noun coupled with the present participle of a verb: the noun gives the personality facet of the subject, the verb the energy facet. For example:

NAME OF SUBJECT	ANALYSIS	
	Personality	Energy
Politics	Community	Organising
Aero Engineering	Aeroplanes	Engineering
Agriculture	Crop	Growing

If we turn to the Decimal Classification we shall find under each class a list of divisions based on the thing itself: on the basic subject. In a few classes (politics is one) no provision has been made for personality divisions, and these are the classes where the classifying of books so often defeats us, forcing us to an unsatisfactory placing. In most classes, however, will be found a series of divisions based on the parts or kinds of the basic subject, and these are the personality divisions. For example:

630 AGRICULTURE

$\left.\begin{array}{l}633\\634\\635\end{array}\right\}$ Crops

629·1 AERO ENGINEERING

$\left.\begin{array}{l}629\cdot133\\629\cdot1343\\629\cdot1344\\629\cdot135\end{array}\right\}$ Types and parts of aircraft

629·2 AUTO ENGINEERING

$\left.\begin{array}{l}629\cdot22\\629\cdot24\\629\cdot25\\629\cdot26\\629\cdot27\\629\cdot28\end{array}\right\}$ Types and parts of automobiles

658 INDUSTRIAL MANAGEMENT
658·9 (with subdivisions drawn from the main schedules) Types of industry.

We have now shown that the Decimal Classification provides divisions for facets relating to each of the fundamental concepts. If we now take any class, and remove successively the sets of divisions relating to the respective fundamental concepts, we shall find that we have taken away all the divisions under that class. In other words, the facet formula is an exhaustive statement of the potential content of any class. For example, in class 630:

630·901 to 630·904 give the divisions relating to time.
630·93 to 630·999 ,, ,, ,, ,, ,, space
631 to 632 ,, ,, ,, ,, ,, energy.
633 to 635 ,, ,, ,, ,, ,, personality.

Matter, as we have already pointed out, is never specified in agriculture. The remaining divisions of 630 (636–7–8–9) are not concerned with agriculture at all, having been squeezed into this class merely because of the limitations of the ten-figure base of the notation.

We must now turn to the question of the order of the set of divisions relating to each facet in the Decimal Classification.

The use of the common subdivision device 09 to introduce the time and space facets automatically throws subjects with foci in these facets to the beginning of a class, when no other facet is specified. They arrange in the order—time, space. Next, each class schedule usually begins with a list of energy divisions, and proceeds afterwards to the matter of personality divisions. It lists its subjects in the actual order in which they will appear on shelves or in catalogues. In other words, it observes the effect of the facet formula:—personality-matter-energy-space-time, which, as we have already shown, by the principle of inversion produces an order of specific subject arrangement just the reverse of the formula. The following examples are drawn from class 630, Agriculture:

630·904 Agriculture in the 20th century	Time only.
630·942084 Agriculture in Britain in the 1930's	Space and time.
631·312 Ploughing	Energy.
631·3120942084 Ploughing in Britain in the 1930's	Energy, space, time.
633·13 Oats	Personality.

From the foregoing examples it can be seen that provision is made for four of the five facets (the fifth, that relating to matter, is never specified in agriculture) in this class of the Decimal Classification, but the structure of the notation will only allow combinations of energy or personality with space and time, never combinations of energy with personality, unless they are actually enumerated in the scheme. Unfortunately, it is combinations of these two facets which are commonest in all subjects, and which give the most highly differentiated subjects.

In theory, it is possible to enumerate under each personality focus all the energy divisions relating to it. In practice, however, it is impossible. This is so because the full number of foci within any facet is unknown, and is always growing. Moreover, the number of known possible combinations is so great that schedules of them would bulk to unwieldy proportions if they were all enumerated. Consequently, wherever enumeration of such derived composites is attempted by the maker of a classification, it must be selective enumeration. This is true of all enumerative schemes. It is for this reason that when we come to classify books by an enumerative scheme we find ourselves confronted with specific divisions in each facet, when what we want is an amalgam of specific divisions drawn from several. We are compelled to make a choice.

It is in this matter of choice that the flair of the classifier has been able to reveal itself in the past. The instinctive classifier has always worked subconsciously within the framework of the facet formula without ever knowing it. The rest of us, and we are in the majority, have had to turn for guidance to what the others have done. We turned to works like Merrill's *Code for classifiers*, which is a list of decisions in specific instances drawn from the practice of certain libraries. This has been the classifier's *vad mecum*. The discipline set out in this present work makes such aids unnecessary.

We have to learn to discern the fundamental concepts at work in the Decimal Classification in order to recognise the divisions of the facet corresponding to each. Space and time, as we have seen, are easily recognised, both as concepts and by their distinctive form of notation. The only serious difficulty comes from energy and personality, and it is on these that we must concentrate our attention. It is hoped that a good selection of examples will demonstrate their working, and hence aid in their recognition.

Before setting out the examples, however, there is one thing we must make clear. Although the Decimal Classification gives ten main classes, this is a purely arbitrary number forced on the scheme by its notation. There are obviously many more main classes. Each of the Decimal Classification main classes must, therefore, be regarded as a bundle of classes tied together in roughly related groups for practical convenience in assigning notation. Glancing through the schedules we can distinguish many more than ten separate classes, each of which requires the separate application of the facet formula. A selection of some of the more obvious classes is:—

150 Psychology; 320 Political science; 330 Economics; 570 Biology; 610 Medicine; 620 Engineering; 669 Metallurgy; 780 Music; 790 Amusements.

Examples of classes in the Decimal Classification with the divisions related to personality and energy separated are given below.

Class		Notation Allocated to Facets	
Name	Number	Personality	Energy
Economic Organisation	338	338·1–·4	338·5–·9
Education	370	372–3–4 376 and 378	371, 375 377, 379
Philology	400	420, 430, 440 450, 460, 470 480, 490–499	421·–8 (in case of English, and similarly 1–8 in other major languages)
Agriculture	630	633–4–5	631, 632
Business	650	658·9 divided according to main scheme	651–659 (excluding 658·9)

CHAPTER X

CANALISATION AND PRACTICAL CLASSIFICATION

WHAT appears in the preceding chapters offers what is perhaps a new approach to classification, but if it cannot be turned to practical use it remains only an interesting theory. To be more than this it must be of day-to-day use to the classifier, and the object of this chapter is to show how this can be so. It is intended to lay down a formal drill for the classifying of books and documentary material which will enable the user to proceed with greater certainty to the correct class number for the item in hand. Those who are instinctive classifiers will say that many of the steps are obvious or unnecessary: they will be quite right. Our method, however, is not aimed at that fortunate few: it is for the many to whom classifying is something of a lottery. It formalises the steps which a good classifier takes intuitively and gives a method of procedure in those cases where experience and intuition fail. For the inexperienced classifier the method is the only means known to us of ensuring a consistent approach to each problem.

So far we have dealt mainly with the principles of construction of a classification: that is to say with making schemes rather than classifying by them. We have tried to show the limitations of enumerative classifications, which proceed by listing all the multifarious specific subjects and then rearranging them in a helpful order, and the advantages of the analytical classification, which assumes a common mould or matrix into which all the many specific subjects can be thrown, and, therefore, makes it unnecessary to know every specific subject.

Thus in constructing an analytical classification it is not necessary to enumerate specific subjects, but only to state the matrix from which the specific subjects can be deduced. This matrix we have called, in accordance with the terminology of Ranganathan, the *facet formula*. The facet formula, we have seen, consists of five facets based on the concepts personality, matter, energy, space and time. The only independent variable in this formula is personality, which determines the specific subject deduced from the matrix. For example, a classification of materials relating to the subject of Packaging would have the following matrix:—Part of package (personality): Material from which made (matter): Manufacturing process or problem (energy): Country (space): Period (time), although the last two would not normally be specified. Now, if provision is made for the representation of any of these facets when it is specified, and for their proper ordering, it is unnecessary to know that there is, for instance, such a specific subject as 'The moulding of glass lids in Belgium in the 19th century,' in order to be able to determine its proper place in the scheme of classification beforehand. Should such a subject arise, we can rest assured that the mechanism of maintaining order will cope with it.

Assuming a classification constructed on such principles, it will be appreciated that classifying will consist of breaking down the specific subject to be classified into terms of the formula, and the assigning of a class number must consist of fitting together according to the rules of the scheme the symbols for each specified part of the formula. In the foregoing example, if MX4 is the class Packaging, Lids is 2, Glass is 5, Moulding is 7, Belgium is 49, and 19th century is 18-, while the connecting device is a point, then the subject 'The moulding of glass lids in Belgium in the 19th century' will be represented by the class mark MX4.2.5.7.49.18-.

In Chapter IX we have shown that the Decimal Classification, although primarily an enumerative scheme, can be thrown into the facet formula in many places. Where we are unable to do this, we may have difficulty in finding specific numbers, or in making a choice between alternative possibilities. The analytical method of classifying, an essential in an analytical scheme, can also be a much more reliable method in an enumerative scheme, because by always observing the same order of facets we shall tend to be consistent in our choice between alternatives.

If we used no analysis at all, we should either have to consult the index for a number every time (until memory made this unnecessary) or we should have to pore over the schedules until we found the name of our subject against a number. In practice both these methods offer grave pitfalls, because a subject can frequently occur in association with more than one area of knowledge. Nevertheless, a specific subject (which we may roughly say is a subject in association with a particular area of knowledge) can have only one proper place in a general scheme of classification. Because of these pitfalls, Sayers and Dewey both warn against using the index of the Decimal Classification for the purpose of classifying. It is wrong, however, to suppose that the index should never be used: it is, in fact, sometimes the only way of knowing where the editors of the Decimal Classification intend certain specific subjects to be placed. The warning should rather be that we take care that we are looking up the *specific* subject; that is, the subject in association with a particular area of knowledge, and to be sure that, of the numbers offered in the index, we choose that which occurs in the associated area of knowledge. In other words, we should take care to choose that number which subsumes our subject under its proper main head.

We suggest that canalisation, or the throwing of a specific subject into the common matrix, eliminates the necessity to rely blindly on memory or on the index, or the more laborious searching through schedules. We suggest also that it enables the placing of unscheduled subjects (that is, subjects for which the scheme makes no provision) at the most appropriate head.

Two things are necessary before the student can use canalisation as a method of classifying by the Decimal Classification. Firstly, he must understand completely the meaning of the facet formula and be able to observe the parts of the formula in a specific subject. Secondly, he must be able to discern the parts of the facet formula in the Decimal Classification.

The object of this book has been to teach students how to reduce subjects to the terms of the fundamental concepts. The fundamental concepts are a generalised statement of the parts of every specific subject and are the basis of Ranganathan's facet formulae. Some attempt has also been made in Chapter IX to set up ghost facet formulae for certain classes of the Decimal

Classification. It is, perhaps, necessary to warn students that the Decimal Classification does not always follow the order of the facet formula, and that they must be prepared to make adjustments and exceptions to accommodate these variants. Sometimes the Decimal Classification variant is so bad that the classifier may well decide to ignore it and to proceed to use a number which is indicated by the facet formula.

An example of such an occasion occurs where the Decimal Classification directs that 'Butchers shops and the meat-selling trade' should be subsumed under the class domestic economy, at 641·4. The facet formula suggests instead, Business Methods (Personality) (Matter) (Energy) (Space) (Time), of which matter, space and time are unspecified, leaving Business Methods (Personality) (Energy). In the context of this class, this gives us Business Methods (kind of business) (business problem), and in this particular case gives Business Methods (meat trade) (unspecified).

Reference to the class 658, Business methods, shows (as is common in the Decimal Classification) a list of divisions based on the energy concept (in this case they are business problems). These extend from 658 to 658·884. At 658·89 and 658·9–999, provision is made for dividing by the personality concept (in this case the kind of business).

Our analysis of the subject showed that the problem (or energy) facet was diffuse, and that therefore we should need no digit to represent it. It remains only to construct a number to represent 'meat trade'. This we do in accordance with the instructions at 658·92–999, and we arrive at the number 658·94136. This is made up thus: 658·9, business methods applied to special businesses; 413 taken from 641·3, meaning food; 6 taken from 636 (as directed at 641·3), meaning meat.

Having begun with a practical demonstration of the value of canalisation as a discipline in classifying, we will now give the essential steps in the drill. Readers are advised to copy these out and keep them to hand in following the worked examples which follow afterwards.

1. Write out the *exact* specific subject of the book to be classified. Break down all composite terms used by the author in

CANALISATION AND PRACTICAL CLASSIFICATION 93

describing the nature of his subject, using a good dictionary and other reference works.

2. Decide whether it is a single- or multi-phased subject.

3. If multi-phased, mark off each phase and determine the nature of the relationship between the phases.

4. From the nature of the relation, determine which is the primary phase.

5. Taking the primary phase first, determine the class to which the subject belongs.

6. Write down the facet formula:—
Class (Personality) (Matter) (Energy) (Space) (Time).

7. Substitute for the general terms of the formula the appropriate terms of the specific subject, putting the word 'diffuse' where a facet is not specified in the subject.

8. Turn up the class in the schedules of the Decimal Classification, and write down the digits which correspond to it.

9. Look in the schedules for that group of division of the class which corresponds with the first facet specified in the formula as set out at 7, and add the appropriate digits to the class number.

10. If the schedule permits subsequent development of the class according to one of the later facets, and such facet is specified in the subject of the book, add the appropriate digits at the end. It will frequently be found that the Decimal Classification appears to offer a choice of two facets, instead of division by both. That is to say that when classifying a subject treating the special specially, choice may have to be made between the general treated specially and the special treated generally, because the classification does not provide for the special treated specially, which is what is required. In such cases, step 7 ensures a correct and consistent choice of the special treated generally.

11. Repeat steps 5–10 for each phase in succession.

12. Complete the class number by assembling the phases using the symbols offered in Supplementary table 2 of the Decimal Classification.

Below are set out examples of subjects of increasing complexity, showing the steps of the drill being applied to each.

94 FUNDAMENTALS OF LIBRARY CLASSIFICATION

Example A. Reid, D. A. G. Building science.
   1. Specific subject—Building.
   2. Single-phased.
   3. N(ot) A(pplicable).
   4. N.A.
   5. Class—Building (In the Decimal Classification this is grouped with Useful Arts).
   6. Building (Personality) (Matter) (Energy) (Space) (Time).
   7. Building (diffuse) (diffuse) (diffuse) (diffuse) (diffuse).
   8. 69.
   9. No facets to be specified by digits, so not applicable.
   10. N.A.
   11. N.A.
   12. Class number—690. (It is a convention in the Decimal Classification that class marks shall consist of a minimum of three digits, the last being a zero when no other is specified: we must therefore add a zero to 69).

Example B. Francis, E.C. Highway arithmetic.
   1. Specific subject—Arithmetic.
   2. Single-phased.
   3. N.A.
   4. N.A.
   5. Class—Science.
   6. Science (P) (M) (E) (S) (T).
   7. Science (arithmetic) (diffuse) (diffuse) (diffuse) (diffuse).
   8. 5.
   9. 511.
   10. N.A.
   11. N.A.
   12. 511—Arithmetic.

Example C. Dickinson, G. Road haulage operation.
   1. Specific subject as title.
   2. Single-phased.
   3. N.A.
   4. N.A.
   5. Business administration.
   6. Business Administration (P) (M) (E) (S) (T).

CANALISATION AND PRACTICAL CLASSIFICATION 95

7. Business Administration (Road transport) (diffuse) (operation) (diffuse) (diffuse).
8. 65.
9. 656. (This is Transport business: it is not possible to specify Road).
10. The schedules do not permit development by the energy characteristic.
11. N.A.
12. The specific subject has to be inadequately represented by the number 656, which only means 'Transport business'.

Example D. British Electricity Authority. Percival Lane (Runcorn) electrical power station.
1. Specific subject as title.
2. Single-phased.
3. and 4. N.A.
5. Electrical Engineering.
6. Electrical Engineering (P) (M) (E) (S) (T).
7. Electrical Engineering (generating plant) (diffuse) (diffuse) (Runcorn) (diffuse).
8. 621·3.
9. 621·312.
10. 621·312094271.
11. N.A.
12. Class number—621·312094271, which means 'Electrical generating plant in Cheshire.'

Example E. Richardson, E. G. Dynamics of real fluids.
1. Specific subject as title.
2. Single-phased.
3. and 4. N.A.
5. Physics.
6. Physics (P) (M) (E) (S) (T).
7. Physics (diffuse) (fluids) (dynamics) (diffuse) (diffuse).
8. 53.
9. 532.
10. 532·5.
11. N.A.
12. 532·5 is Dynamics of fluids.

Example F. Baker, L. The design of marine water tube boilers.
 1. Specific subject as title.
 2. Single-phased.
 3. and 4. N.A.
 5. Engineering.
 6. Engineering (P) (M) (E) (S) (T).
 7. Engineering (marine boilers) (diffuse) (design) (diffuse) (diffuse).
 8. 62.
 9. 621·18422.
 10. No provision in the schedules for provision according to the energy characteristic.
 11. N.A.
 12. Class number—621·18422, which means 'Marine boilers.'
We are forced to ignore the focus Design in the energy facet.

Example G. Whittick, A. European architecture in the twentieth century.
 1. Specific subject as title.
 2. Single-phased.
 3. and 4. N.A.
 5. Architecture.
 6. Architecture (P) (M) (E) (S) (T).
 7. Architecture (diffuse) (diffuse) (diffuse) (Europe) (20th century).
 8. 72.
 9. 720·94.
 10. 720·9405.
 11. N.A.
 12. Class number—720·9405, which means 'European architecture in the 20th century.'

(The Decimal Classification gives a schedule for styles of architecture, including twentieth century style, which may be divided by country. Since this work is a history of architecture and not necessarily a study of the twentieth century style, the normal space divisions are preferred.)

Example H. Bower, M. The development of executive leadership.
 1. Specific subject as title.

2. Single-phased.
3. and 4. N.A.
5. Class—Business Administration.
6. Business Administration (P) (M) (E) (S) (T).
7. Business Administration (diffuse) (diffuse) (executive staffs) (diffuse) (diffuse).
8. 65.
9. 651·372.
10. and 11. N.A.
12. Class number—651·372, which means 'Executive staffs in business administration.'

Example I. Bellamy, H. S. Moons, myths and men.
1. Specific subject—Theories of the moon and their influence on mythology.
2. Two-phased.
3. The two phases are 1. Moon, 2. Mythology.
4. The kind of phase is the 'influencing phase.' (i.e. influence of moon theories on mythology) and the primary phase is the subject influenced (i.e. mythology). The linking symbol is 0001.
5. *Primary phase* Class—Religion (The Decimal Classification puts mythology under 29, Other religions).
6. Religion (P) (M) (E) (S) (T).
7. Religion (myths) (diffuse) (diffuse) (diffuse) (diffuse).
8. 2.
9. 291·13.
10. N.A.
11. Step 5 for *secondary phase* Class—Astronomy.
    6. Astronomy (P) (M) (E) (S) (T).
    7. Astronomy (moon) (diffuse) (diffuse) (diffuse) (diffuse).
    8. 52.
    9. 523·3.
    10. N.A.
12. Class number—291·1300015233, which means 'The moon in relation to mythology'. This is the nearest we can get to the specific subject, as the phase links in the Decimal Classification do not identify the phases.

Example J. Knight M. Spiritualism, reincarnation and immortality.

1. Specific subject—The Christian doctrine of conditional immortality compared with the spiritualist doctrine of survival after death. (The portion of the book which deals with reincarnation is found to be negligible.)
2. Two-phased.
3. The two phases are 1. conditional immortality, 2. survival after death.
4. The kind of phase is the 'comparison phase'. With the comparison phase there is no rule for determining the order of the phases in every case. In the work we are classifying the writer is concerned with showing the superiority of the Christian doctrine, and we therefore select this as the primary phase.
5. *Primary phase* Class—Religion.
6. Religion (P) (M) (E) (S) (T).
7. Religion (Christianity) (diffuse) (conditional immortality) (diffuse) (diffuse).
8. 2.
9. and 10. 237·3. (N.B. 23 is Christian doctrine, and 237 is future state. There is no separate number for Christianity: the personality and energy divisions are fused.)
11. Step 5 for *secondary phase* Class—Transcendental Psychology and Occult Sciences (we shall shorten this to Transcendental Psychology for convenience).

> Step 6. Transcendental Psychology (P) (M) (E) (S) (T).
> 7. Transcendental Psychology (Spiritualism) (diffuse) (survival) (diffuse) (diffuse).
> 8. 133.
> 9. 133·9.
> 10. Survival not specified in schedules.

12. Class number—237·300011339, which means Christian doctrine of immortality in relation to spiritualism. This is the nearest we can get to the specific subject, as one facet of spiritualism is not scheduled, and the phase links do not identify the phases.

CANALISATION AND PRACTICAL CLASSIFICATION 99

Example K. Turkevich, L. B. Cervantes in Russia.
1. Specific subject—The influence of Cervantes's literary work on Russian literature.
2. Two-phased.
3. The two phases are 1, Cervantes's literary work, 2. Russian literature.
4. The kind of phase is the influencing phase, and the primary phase is the subject influenced. The linking symbol is 0001.
5. *Primary phase* Class—Literature.
6. Literature (P) (M) (E) (S) (T).
7. Literature (Russian) (diffuse) (diffuse) (diffuse) (diffuse).
8. 8.
9. 891·7.
10. N.A.
11. Step 5 for *secondary phase* Class—Literature.
    6. Literature (P) (M) (E) (S) (T).
    7. Literature (Cervantes) (diffuse) (diffuse) (diffuse) (diffuse).
8. 8.
9. 863·32.
10. N.A.
12. Class number—891·7000186332, which means Russian literature in relation to Cervantes. This is the nearest we can get to the specific subject, as the phase links do not identify the phases.

(Note on example K. The personality of literature inheres in the country and period of origin, which are prime factors in producing the authors who are the ultimate personification of the class literature. This is true of the arts generally.)

In using this discipline it will be found again and again that the Decimal Classification fails to individualise specific subjects. This is due to two main factors: failure to supply sufficient personality divisions (cf. 320 and 656), and failure to allow for the coupling of matter or energy divisions to any one of a number of personality divisions (cf. 370 and 635·9).

We have stated that classifying should cease when the most specific number consistent with the facet formula has been reached. We have seen that such a method may leave a great

G*

deal of unclassified material at a general head. What can be done to break this down? We cannot use any symbols of the classification, because we do not know which symbols may later be used for the same purpose by the central editing committee. We can only add the missing part in words, thus:

656 [Timetable planning]

The obvious advantage of this is that in the catalogue (though not on the shelves) we can make further subdivisions under an undeveloped head.

We cannot engage in unlimited systematic arrangement of verbal extensions to class numbers because they cannot be indexed, since the only possible way to index systematic arrangement is to give it a notation. We seem to be up against an insoluble problem, and it must be emphasised that it is a problem that can only be satisfactorily settled when the maker of the scheme either provides an expansion of the subject concerned, or transmits to the classifier more autonomy in number building.

CHAPTER XI

THE CHAIN PROCEDURE FOR SUBJECT INDEXING AND FEATURING

THE claim of the classified catalogue is that under any given head it lays out the divisions and subdivisions of a subject in a useful and intelligible order so that once a reader has arrived at the section of the catalogue appropriate to his interest the order of the scheme itself assists him.

The normal user of the library, however, has little or no knowledge of classification schemes, and must be helped to find the appropriate place by some convenient auxiliary apparatus. What is needed is an index which will guide him from the natural name of the subject to the artificial name (i.e. class number) irrespective of the natural language in which the approach is first made, and so put him in a position to take advantage of the systematic arrangement provided by the classification scheme. This includes the benefit of the facility of approaching *via* a wider or narrower subject than the one actually required. Thus, although the actual content of the specific subject sought may not be fully appreciated, the layout of the field of knowledge in which the reader finds himself as a result of consulting the index assists him to a better understanding of his own requirements. In Chapter II (p. 24) we discussed the habits of readers in this respect.

We require, then, a system which will index specific subjects, the more general subject which comprehends them, and the even more general subject which in turn comprehends that. For example, the subject *virus diseases of potatoes* might be sought under any of the following headings:

Virus diseases of potatoes.
Diseases, virus, of potatoes.
Potatoes, virus diseases of.
Potatoes. Diseases, Virus.
Root crops. Potatoes, virus diseases of.

Root crops: virus diseases of potatoes.
Agriculture. Potatoes, virus diseases of.
Agriculture. Potatoes. Diseases, virus.

These represent but a small selection of the many possible combinations of the various terms which together constitute the natural name of the specific subject. Such profusion of entries is clearly uneconomic, and in practice a selection has to be made. The question arises, must this selection be left to the flair of the individual cataloguer, or is it possible to lay down a discipline which will enable a cataloguer to select from this galaxy of choice those entries which are vital, but which in themselves give an exhaustive enumeration of the words under which the subject may be sought?

In order to discover a basis, let us first assume an index in which the profusion of entries suggested above has been provided in full. Under Agriculture there will appear an incomplete yet nevertheless enormous series of entries variously subheaded potatoes, diseases, virus diseases, field crops, root crops, and a thousand and one other. The reader who, requiring information on the virus diseases of potatoes, looks under agriculture has still to make a search for his specific subject which may be under any one of several subheadings, and he has no guarantee under which it will be found.

In effect, the index would be here using the alphabet to narrow the field of selection within the class agriculture on a haphazard basis, *whereas the task has already been carried out systematically by the classification scheme*. The systematic order of the classification clearly relieves us, therefore, of the necessity to proceed from the general to the specific in any entry in the index. Thus, the only entry required under agriculture in this case is a general one which will refer the reader to the classified catalogue or to the shelves for a display of all the subjects subsumed under it.

We shall find it equally profitable to apply the same principle to the other combinations of terms. Field crops is a subject which comprehends not only potatoes and other root crops, but cereals and forage crops, etc. To seek virus diseases of potatoes under field crops is again to be forced to the more specific

CHAIN PROCEDURE FOR INDEXING AND FEATURING   103

through the medium of alphabetical order which, as we have already seen, is haphazard, and merely does again the task already better done by the system of the classification.

We can see from these examples that, because the classification lays out under any general subject the specific parts of that subject, there is no need when indexing that general subject to set out again the specific parts as subheadings under it.

Let us now apply this to some examples in the Decimal Classification.

Example A. Cultivation of potatoes   Step 1
      Class number 633·491   „ 2
Digit-by-digit translation of the class number
Agriculture—fieldcrops—roots crops—tubers=potatoes   „ 3
Entries required to give an exhaustive enumeration of the vital components of the name of the subject.   „ 4
    POTATOES. *AGRICULTURE*   633·491
    TUBERS. *AGRICULTURE*   633·49
    ROOT CROPS. *AGRICULTURE*   633·4
    FIELD CROPS. *AGRICULTURE*   633
    AGRICULTURE   630

Example B.
  1. Sales promotion.
  2. 658·82
  3. Business-management-selling-trade promotion.
  4. TRADE PROMOTION. *BUSINESS*   658·82
     SELLING. *BUSINESS*   658·8
     MANAGEMENT. *BUSINESS*   658
     BUSINESS   650

Example C.
  1. Cartoon drawing.
  2. 741·5.
  3. Fine arts-drawing-illustration-cartoons.
  4. CARTOONS. *DRAWING*   741·5
     ILLUSTRATION. *DRAWING*   741
     DRAWING. *FINE ARTS*   740
     FINE ARTS   700

It will have been observed that the most specific part of a subject classified by the Decimal Classification is that reflected by the extreme right-hand part of the class number. In example A, the digit 1 represents potatoes, in example B, the digit 2 represents trade promotion, and in example C, the digit 5 represents cartoons. It must be obvious, therefore, that if the notation is properly constructed the digits represent more and more general ideas as we read them from right to left; that is, from back to front. If, then, the concepts indicated by the notation are indexed at each step as the class number is denuded of successive digits, a chain of subjects of increasing generality will have been indexed. Indeed this is what has happened in each of the three examples. This is the basis of the chain procedure for arriving at the subject index entries to be raised for any Decimal Classification number.

At first, because of the faults in construction of the Decimal Classification, the resulting headings may appear clumsy, but it is essential to persist with this method until the discipline is established. Once the correct procedure is firmly grasped, the incongruities which arise from the awkwardness of the classification scheme will be thrown up, and can be smoothed out.

The discipline also proves an infallible check on the correctness of the main class chosen by the classifier, being a mechanisation of Sayers' instruction to classifiers to read up to the main heading when a placing has been selected. Care must be taken to use the terms represented by the separate digits of the class number. If, as a result of this, the heading fails to subsume the subject under the correct main class, then a fresh attempt must be made to find the proper main class. The chain must never be 'moulded' to fit in with the classifier's own preconceptions. There are, unfortunately, some absurdities in the Decimal Classification which cannot be evaded: for example, the subsuming of 'thieves slang' under 'welfare organisations'.

Difficulties are bound to arise, however, in applying such a strict discipline to the Decimal Classification. Some of the most important are given below, with the method of dealing with each.

1. The terms in the schedules may be found to be archaic, American, or insufficiently precise. In such cases, substitute

CHAIN PROCEDURE FOR INDEXING AND FEATURING 105

synonyms of a more suitable kind. All normal synonyms must be indexed and one of them chosen as the basis of the chain.

2. The first term of the first heading may be found to be a common subdivision under which no one would be likely to consult the index. This proves a very difficult problem in working with the Decimal Classification, because the same symbols have not been used consistently to represent the same common subdivisions. Had such been the case, a general reference of the type:—

> DESIGN for Design applied to any subject SEE under the number for that subject, amplified by the number 0034.

would have sufficed. As it is, the only real remedy would appear to be a somewhat non-committal reference of the type:—

> DESIGN for Design applied to any subject SEE under the number for that subject.

3. The schedules may be found to contain headings of no particular significance so that a digit-by-digit translation of a class number into appropriate words may contain a number of redundant or repetitive terms (for example, 'General questions'). This is a most irritating fault in the Decimal Classification, and such completely redundant heads must be ignored in the chain. For example:—621·381 Electric communication: general. Clearly 621·38 is the general head, and the extra digit 1 serves no useful purpose.

4. The schedules may not be developed as far as the specific subject to be indexed. This frequent fault is common to all enumerative schemes of classification. We saw, in Chapter X, that it gave rise to ambiguity in classification, and we have laid down a formula for resolving the difficulty in classifying any particular item. Though we may not be able to individualise a subject by a class number, we must make provision in our index for the part of the subject not expressed by the class number. The method is to add to the right hand side of the class number the word not expressed by that number: for example,

791·4 [Cinema]

and to begin the chain of references from the verbal extension.

Featuring

The index tells the reader in which part of the classification he should look for the subject he is seeking. In the case of the classified catalogue, the 'entry words' are numbers and the meanings of these are not readily apparent to the reader, so that he cannot perceive unaided the layout of his subject. The cataloguer should, therefore, assist him to utilise the systematic arrangement of the classification scheme by writing the meaning against each class number.

Taking the examples given above, we find that the digit-by-digit translation of the class number requires considerable space, so that it will obviously be uneconomic and confusing to give a full translation of each number. Some principle of reduction, similar to the principle sought in chain procedure indexing must be found. Consider example A, 633·491, Cultivation of potatoes. A full translation, digit-by-digit, gives Agriculture—field crops—root crops—tubers—potatoes.

It is highly probable that there will already exist in the catalogue entries for works on some of the more general subjects: agriculture and root crops, for example. The reader examining entries in the part of the catalogue dealing with field crops will be aware of the agricultural context, and will not, therefore, need to be reminded of it on every entry. Similarly with the entries dealing with root crops: he will not need to be reminded of field crops and agriculture on every entry: he infers them from the context.

This indicates that, provided a translation is made at every step, whether or not any entry exists there at a given moment, the only digit of a class number which needs to be translated is that on the extreme right. The translation of the notational entry word in this manner is known as *featuring*. The British National Bibliography is featured and indexed in accordance with the methods described in this chapter.

Only the barest outline of the discipline for chain procedure subject indexing and featuring has been given, but it is hoped that any cataloguer who understands and adopts the principles set out in this book will be able to develop the two disciplines in practice. In this way he will find himself relieved of many of the anxieties and uncertainties which have beset cataloguers in the past. His work will be governed by a body of principles which conceive cataloguing and classifications as symbiotic techniques.

CHAPTER XII

CONCLUSION, WITH A NOTE OF OUTSTANDING PROBLEMS IN CLASSIFICATION

WE have been led to the writing of this book by several circumstances, not the least being the attitude of many of our colleagues who take the view that classification is doing its job so long as it provides a book with a number to index. This is simply not true: classification turns on order, and unless a scheme enables a subject to be set in its appropriate place within an order, that scheme fails. Unless, too, classifiers in different places at different times put a subject in the same appointed place for the same sort of library, they fail as technicians. Yet we know that such failures are common. We believe that we have learned a discipline which is effective in securing consistency in classifying, and we have endeavoured to impart it.

Owing to limitations of space, this book has had to be suggestive rather than exhaustive; but there are other works which will amplify our theme, notably those of Ranganathan. Readers who grasp firmly the discipline we propose will find it a great aid in classifying by any scheme. It cannot be denied, however, that there will be practical difficulties in applying such a rigid discipline to the Decimal Classification, which is compounded of a series of often unco-ordinated *ad hoc* classifications for special subjects, particularly in the 14th edition, which was no longer controlled by the genius of Dewey himself. These difficulties have to be faced: some indication of them has been given in this present work.

The effect on us of our study has been to disclose and underline definite reasons for the general complaint of all librarians that Decimal Classification proves daily more inadequate to our needs.

We have shown that, though the divisions of this scheme are based on the five fundamental concepts, the notation does not allow the assembly of divisions from the personality, matter and energy facets. And though it may be feasible to reconstruct the Decimal Classification so as to make it a faceted scheme, yet the separation of related fields of interest such as sociology and history, and the association of unrelated ones such as sociology and statistics would remain; so also would the restriction to ten so-called main classes which imposes a long notation on many classes (e.g. psychology, business administration). Moreover, the result of the rearrangement of notation would be to destroy the present Decimal Classification numbers, necessitating the complete reclassification of existing stocks. This being so, we should do better to start again with a new classification which would follow the principles found to underlie modern schemes when they are functioning at their best.

It has been the main purpose of our study to lay bare the principles upon which a classification scheme should be constructed: it must give a helpful order, it must fix that order and preserve it by means of a notation, it must offer infinite hospitality in chain and array, and it must allow maximum autonomy to the classifier. We find that the only scheme produced so far which comes within measurable distance of this ideal is the Colon Classification of Ranganathan. This generation must face its responsibilities: a new classification scheme is urgently needed, and must be produced. It may take the form of an entirely new scheme, or a remodelling or development of an existing one. We suggest that, as a piece of urgent research, the Colon Classification should be studied with a view to increasing its usefulness in the Western industrial civilisation, and to developing its techniques. It may save building anew from the ground up.

Chain procedure and featuring deserve far more attention than the rather scanty treatment of one chapter which we have been able to spare for them. This niggardliness was due to our acceptance of the commonly held belief that there are two separate but related studies: classification and cataloguing. We now realise, as a result of concentration upon problems in writing this book, that these two are symbiotic. There is really only one subject, the organisation of knowledge. Their separation was due to the uneven pace at which they have developed. Classification lost ground as a means of arranging catalogues because existing schemes could not grow as fast as knowledge, and so was relegated to the rask of arranging the physical books, the task of organising the knowledge in them being given to the dictionary catalogue. Their separation of function led to the study of each in relation only to the task it was performing.

The organisation of knowledge demands a system of arrangement of materials which will observe the scientific and educational consensus in its grouping of major fields of knowledge, and which will store material in each group in a prescribed and intelligible order. It should permit an approach to be made to specific subjects from any level in the hierarchy, and the order itself should be such as to lead readily to super-ordinate or subordinate subjects.

To the preferred systematic arrangement chosen as the basis of the principal part of the catalogue must be added the following:

(1) An alphabetical key to the subjects which will lead into the materials in the systematic arrangement at the exact level of approach and which will list all the distributed facets.

(2) An alphabetical arrangement which will enable a specific book to be found of which the author, title or series is known.

Outstanding Problems and Matters for Investigation

1. Examine main classes from the point of view of fields of interest. Bliss has already done much of this work.

2. Examine the problem of facet formulas for the principal fields of interest, particularly the fine arts and industrial arts.

3. Examine the phenomenon of phase relation, and define phases and their relative positions in the hierarchy of a subject.

4. Examine the question of common subdivisions in relation to (a) the facet formula. (Some common subdivisions in present schemes are only common foci of the energy facets.) (b) form divisions. (The old confusion between inner and outer form needs clearing up, so that form proper can be given its correct place in the hierarchy of the subjects.)

5. Examine various kinds of notation and the relative usefulness of different species.

6. Examine the problem of main class notation in regard to the problem of collocating new co-ordinate classes.

7. Examine the possibility of seminal mnemonics (or seminal constants, as they might be less ambiguously termed).

8. Examine the possibility of shortening notation.

9. Examine the possibility of expressing partial comprehension of multi-focal facets.

BIBLIOGRAPHY

It would be pointless for us to list all the books which have gone to the making of this study, since it would resolve itself into a bibliography of classification and cataloguing, already adequately done elsewhere. However, some works have had more influence than others, and these are listed below.

BLISS, Henry Evelyn. A bibliographic classification, extended by systematic auxiliary schedules for composite specification and notation. . . . New York, H. W. Wilson, 1940 ——v.

BLISS, Henry Evelyn. The organisation of knowledge and the system of the sciences . . . . New York, H. Holt, 1929.

BLISS, Henry Evelyn. The organisation of knowledge in libraries and the subject-approach to books, 2nd ed., rev. and partly re-written. New York, H. W. Wilson, 1939.

RANGANATHAN, Shiyali Ramarita. Classification and international documentation. (In Review of Documentation, Vol. XVII, Fasc. 2, 1947. pp. 154–77.)

RANGANATHAN, Shiyali Ramarita. Elements of library classification, based on lectures delivered at the University of Bombay in December, 1944. Poona, N. K. Publishing House, 1945.

RANGANATHAN, Shiyali Ramarita. Library classification: fundamentals and procedure, with 1008 graded examples and exercises . . . . Madras, Madras Library Association, 1937.

RANGANATHAN, Shiyali Ramarita. Prolegomena to library classification. Madras, Madras Library Association, 1937.

SAYERS, William Charles Berwick. An introduction to library classification; theoretical, historical and practical, with readings, exercises and examination papers. 7th ed., rev. London, Grafton, 1944.

SAYERS, William Charles Berwick. A manual of classification for libraries and bibliographers. 2nd ed., rev. London, Grafton, 1944.

INDEX

Alphabet. Notation symbols, 61, 63
   Flexibility, 71–72
Alphabetical index, 101–105
Alphabetical *versus* systematic order of subjects, 21
Analytical method of classifying, 90
Arbitrary signs. Notation symbols, 61
   Flexibility, 72
Array and chain. Examples, 39
Author arrangement. Evaluation, 18–19
Autonomy for the classifier, 76–81

Bias phase, 55, 59
Bliss, H. E. Viewpoint in classification, 13
   Consensus, 23
   Order of arrangement, 25
   Co-extensiveness, 62

Canalisation, 89–100
Chain and array. Examples, 39
Chain procedure, 101–105
Characteristics of division. Succession, 29
Class numbers. Featuring, 106
Classification. Purpose, 17–18
Classified catalogue. Parts, 110
   Usefulness of systematic order, 101
Classifying. Technique, 92
Coextensive *versus* brief notation, 62
Common subdivisions, 76–77
Comparison phase, 56, 59
Consistent classifying. How to ensure, 89
Coordinate classes. Possible orders, 29
Cross division, 30

Decimal classification. Index, Use and limitations of, 90
   Main classes, Arbitrary nature of, 87
   Notation, Failure of, 50
   Reconstruction of, 108
Decimal notation, 68
Dictionary *versus* classified catalogue, 109
Division, 35–41

Energy facet. Definition, 37
   In the Decimal Classification, 83
Enumerative classification. Definition, 37
   Inability to expand helpfully, 76
Extension and intension, 25–26

Facet analysis. Decimal Classification. Examples, 31, 38
   Definition, 32
Facet and phase. Distinction, 58
Facet formula. Application, 90
Faceted classification. Method of construction, 37
Faceted notation, 71
Facets. Collective expression of complete class, 85
Facets. Decimal Classification, Combination not possible in, 86
   Examples, 31
   Notation, 64
   Order, 86
   Definition, 31
Featuring, 106–107
Form phase, 55, 59
Fundamental concepts, 42
   In Decimal Classification, 44
   Order, 47

Helpful order, 23–34
   In array, 51
   In chain, 52

Hospitality in array. Notation, 69
Hospitality in chain. Notation. 68–69

Index, 101–105
Indicator digits. Definition, 65
Indicator digits in the major schemes, 59
Influence phase, 56, 59
Integer notation, 68
Inverse order, Principle of, 50

Matter facet. Definition, 43–44
    In Decimal Classification, 84
Mnemonics, 76–81

Notation, 60–75

Octave device, 70
Organisation of knowledge, 109–110

Personality facet. Definition, 84
    In Decimal Classification, 85
Phase, 53–59
Phase analysis. Examples, 57
Phase and facet. Distinction, 58
Phase indicators, 59
Phases. Decimal Classification. Notation, 64
Preferred order, 74
Primary phase, 57

Ranganathan, S. R. Order in array, 29
    Principle of inverse order, 51
    Fundamental concepts, 42

Ranganathan,
    Phase analysis, 58
    Co-extensiveness, 62
    Unscheduled mnemonics, 80
Relationships revealed by classification, 36
Relative location, 68
Research projects, 110

Sayers, W. C. B. Extension and intension, 26
    Use of index, 91
    Checking method, 104
Seminal mnemonics, 78
Space facet in Decimal Classification, 83
Specific subject. Definition, 90
Subject approach, 19
Subject headings. Choice of terms, 102
Symbiosis of classification and cataloguing, 109
Symbols. Notation, 60–66

Terms. Difficulties, 46
Time facet in Decimal Classification, 82
Title arrangement. Evaluation, 19
Tool phase, 56, 59

Verbal extensions, 105

For Product Safety Concerns and Information please contact our EU representative GPSR@taylorandfrancis.com
Taylor & Francis Verlag GmbH, Kaufingerstraße 24, 80331 München, Germany